Ngũgĩ wa Thiong'o is Distinguished Professor of English and Comparative Literature at the University of California, Irvine, and is director of the university's International Centre for Writing and Translation. His books include *Petals of Blood*, for which he was imprisoned by the Kenyan government in 1977, and *Wizard of the Crow*, which was published by Harvill Secker to great acclaim in 2006. He lives in Irvine, California.

NGŨGĨ WA THIONG'O

Dreams in a Time of War

A Childhood Memoir

VINTAGE BOOKS
London

Published by Vintage 2011

2 4 6 8 10 9 7 5 3 1

Copyright © Ngũgĩ wa Thiong'o 2010

Ngũgĩ wa Thiong'o has asserted his right under the Copyright, Designs
and Patents Act 1988 to be identified as the author of this work

First published in Great Britain in 2010 by Harvill Secker

Vintage
Random House, 20 Vauxhall Bridge Road,
London SW1V 2SA

www.vintage-books.co.uk

Addresses for companies within The Random House Group Limited
can be found at: www.randomhouse.co.uk/offices.htm

The Random House Group Limited Reg. No. 954009

A CIP catalogue record for this book
is available from the British Library

ISBN 9780099548522

This book has been selected to receive financial assistance from
English PEN's Writers in Translation programme supported by
Bloomberg. English PEN exists to promote literature and its
understanding, uphold writer's freedoms around the world,
campaign against the persecution and imprisonment of writers
for stating their views, and promote the friendly co-operation
of writers and free exchange of ideas

The Random House Group Limited supports The Forest
Stewardship Council (FSC), the leading international forest
certification organisation. All our titles that are printed on
Greenpeace approved FSC certified paper carry the FSC logo.
Our paper procurement policy can be found at:
www.rbooks.co.uk/environment

Mixed Sources
Product group from well-managed
forests and other controlled sources
www.fsc.org   Cert no. TT-COC-2139
© 1996 Forest Stewardship Council

FSC

Printed and bound in Great Britain by
CPI Cox & Wyman, Reading, RG1 8EX

For Thiong'o senior, Kĩmunya, Ndũcũ, Mũkoma, Wanjikũ, Njoki, Bjorn, Mũmbi, Thiong'o K, and niece Ngĩna in the hope that your children will read this and get to know their great-grandmother Wanjikũ and great-uncle Wallace Mwangi, a.k.a. Good Wallace, and the role they played in shaping our dreams; for the entire Ndũcũ clan and Thiong'o family and for my wife Njeeri wa Ngũgĩ who urged me to write this memoir.

Wanjikũ wa Ngũgĩ, the author's mother

There is nothing like a dream to create the future.

—VICTOR HUGO, *Les Misérables*

I have learnt
from books dear friend
of men dreaming and living
and hungering in a room without a light
who could not die since death was far too poor
who did not sleep to dream, but dreamed to change the world.

—MARTIN CARTER, "Looking at Your Hands"

In the dark times
Will there also be singing?
Yes, there will be singing
About the dark times.

—BERTOLT BRECHT, "Motto"

Dreams in a
Time of War

Years later when I read T. S. Eliot's line that April was the cruelest month, I would recall what happened to me one April day in 1954, in chilly Limuru, the prime estate of what, in 1902, another Eliot, Sir Charles Eliot, then governor of colonial Kenya, had set aside as White Highlands. The day came back to me, the now of it, vividly.

I had not had lunch that day, and my tummy had forgotten the porridge I had gobbled that morning before the six-mile run to Kĩnyogori Intermediate School. Now there were the same miles to cross on my way back home; I tried not to look too far ahead to a morsel that night. My mother was pretty good at conjuring up a meal a day, but when one is hungry, it is better to find something, anything, to take one's mind away from thoughts of food. It was what I often did at lunchtime when other kids took out the food they had brought and those who dwelt in the neighborhood went home to eat during the midday break. I would often pretend that I was going someplace, but really it was to any shade of a tree or cover of a bush, far from the other kids, just to read a book, any book, not that there were many of them, but even class notes were a welcome distraction. That day I read from the abridged version of Dickens's *Oliver Twist*. There was a line drawing of Oliver Twist, a bowl in hand, looking up to a towering figure, with the caption "Please sir, can I have some more?" I identified with that question; only for me it was often directed at my mother, my sole benefactor, who always gave more whenever she could.

Listening to stories and anecdotes from the other kids was also a soothing distraction, especially during the walk back home, a lesser ordeal than in the morning when we had to run barefoot to school, all the way, sweat streaming down our cheeks, to avoid tardiness and the inevitable lashes on our open palms. On the way home, except for those kids from Ndeiya or Ngeca who had to cover ten miles or more, the walk was more leisurely. It was actually better so, killing time on the road before the evening meal of uncertain regularity or chores in and around the home compound.

Kenneth, my classmate, and I used to be quite good at killing time, especially as we climbed the last hill before home. Facing the sloping side, we each would kick a "ball," mostly Sodom apples, backward over our heads up the hill. The next kick would be from where the first ball had landed, and so on, competing to beat each other to the top. It was not the easiest or fastest way of getting there, but it had the virtue of making us forget the world. But now we were too big for that kind of play. Besides, no games could beat storytelling for capturing our attention.

We often crowded around whoever was telling a tale, and those who were really good at it became heroes of the moment. Sometimes, in competing for proximity to the narrator, one group would push him off the main path to one side; the other group would shove him back to the other side, the entire lot zigzagging along like sheep.

This evening was no different, except for the route we took. From Kĩnyogori to my home village, Kwangũgĩ or Ngamba, and its neighborhoods we normally took a path that went through a series of ridges and valleys, but when listening to a tale, one did not notice the ridge and fields of corn, potatoes, peas, and beans, each field bounded by wattle trees or hedges of kei apple and gray thorny bushes. The path eventually led to the Kĩhingo area, past my old elementary school, Manguo, down the valley, and then up a hill of grass and black wattle trees. But today, following, like sheep, the lead teller of tales, we took another route, slightly longer, along the fence of the Limuru Bata Shoe factory, past its stinking dump site of rubber debris and rotting hides and skins, to a junction of railway tracks and roads, one of which led to the marketplace. At the crossroads was a crowd of men and women, probably coming from market, in animated discussion. The crowd grew larger as workers from the shoe factory also stopped and joined in. One or two boys recognized some relatives in the crowd. I followed them, to listen.

"He was caught red-handed," some were saying.

"Imagine, bullets in his hands. In broad daylight."

Everybody, even we children, knew that for an African to be caught with bullets or empty shells was treason; he would be dubbed a terrorist, and his hanging by the rope was the only outcome.

"We could hear gunfire," some were saying.

"I saw them shoot at him with my own eyes."

"But he didn't die!"

"Die? Hmm! Bullets flew at those who were shooting."

"No, he flew into the sky and disappeared in the clouds."

Disagreements among the storytellers broke the crowd into smaller groups of threes, fours, and fives around a narrator with his own perspective on what had taken place that afternoon. I found myself moving from one group to another, gleaning bits here and there. Gradually I pieced together strands of the story, and a narrative of what bound the crowd emerged, a riveting tale about a nameless man who had been arrested near the Indian shops.

The shops were built on the ridge, rows of buildings that faced each other, making for a huge rectangular enclosure for carriages and shoppers, with entrance-exits at the corners. The ridge sloped down to a plain where stood African-owned buildings, again built to form a similar rectangle, the enclosed space often used as a market on Wednesdays and Saturdays. The goats and sheep for sale on the same two market days were tethered in groups in the large sloping space between the two sets of shopping centers. That area had apparently been the theater of action that now animated the group of narrators and listeners. They all agreed that after handcuffing the man, the police put him in the back of their truck.

Suddenly, the man had jumped out and run. Caught unawares, the police turned the truck around and chased the man, their guns aimed at him. Some of them jumped out and pursued him on foot. He mingled with shoppers and then ran through a gap between two shops into the open space between the Indian and African shops. Here, the police opened fire. The man would fall, but only to rise again and run from side to side. Time and again this had happened, ending only with the man's zigzagging his way through the herds of sheep and goats, down the slopes, past the African shops, across the rails, to the other side, past the crowded workers' quarters of the Limuru Bata Shoe Company, up the ridge till he disappeared, apparently unharmed, into the European-owned lush green tea plantations. The chase had turned the hunted, a man without a name, into an instant legend, inspiring numerous tales of heroism and magic among those who had witnessed the event and others who had received the story secondhand.

I had heard similar stories about Mau Mau guerrilla fighters, Dedan Kĩmathi in particular; only, until then, the magic had happened far away in Nyandarwa and the Mount Kenya mountains, and the tales were never told by anybody who had been an eyewitness. Even my friend Ngandi, the most informed teller of tales, never said that he had actually seen any of the actions he described so graphically. I love listening more than telling, but this was the one story I was eager to tell, before or after the meal. Next time I met Ngandi, I could maybe hold my own.

The X-shaped barriers to the railway crossing level were raised. A siren sounded, and the train passed by, a reminder to the crowd that they still had miles to go. Kenneth and I followed suit, and when no longer in the company of the other students he spoiled the mood by contesting the veracity of the story, at least the manner in which it had been told. Kenneth liked a clear line between fact and fiction; he did not relish the two mixed. Near his place, we parted without having agreed on the degree of exaggeration.

Home at last, to my mother, Wanjikũ, and my younger brother, Njinjũ, my sister Njoki, and my elder brother's wife, Charity. They were huddled together around the fireside. Despite Kenneth, I was still giddy with the story of the man without a name, like one of those characters in books. Sudden pangs of hunger brought me back to earth. But it was past dusk, and that meant an evening meal might soon be served.

Food was ready all right, handed to me in a calabash bowl, in total silence. Even my younger brother, who liked to call out my failings, such as my coming home after dusk, was quiet. I wanted to explain why I was late, but first I had to quell the rumbling in my tummy.

In the end, my explanation was not necessary. My mother broke the silence. Wallace Mwangi, my elder brother, Good Wallace as he was popularly known, had earlier that afternoon narrowly escaped death. We pray for his safety in the mountains. It is this war, she said.

I was born in 1938, under the shadow of another war, the Second World War, to Thiong'o wa Ndũcũ, my father, and Wanjikũ wa Ngũgĩ, my mother. I don't know where I ranked, in terms of years, among the twenty-four children of my father and his four wives, but I was the fifth child of my mother's house. Ahead of me were the eldest sister, Gathoni; eldest brother, Wallace Mwangi; and sisters Njoki and Gacirũ, in that order, with my younger brother, Njinjũ, being the sixth and last born of my mother.

My earliest recollection of home was of a large courtyard, five huts forming a semicircle. One of these was my father's, where goats also slept at night. It was the main hut not because of its size but because it was set apart and equidistant from the other four. It was called a *thingira*. My father's wives, or our mothers as we called them, would take food to his hut in turns.

Each woman's hut was divided into spaces with different functions, a three-stone fireplace at its center; sleeping areas and a kind of pantry; a large section for goats and, quite often, a small enclosure, a pen for fattening sheep or goats to be slaughtered for special occasions. Each household had a granary, a small round hut on stilts, with walls made of thin sticks woven together. The granary was a measure of plenty and dearth. After a good harvest, it would be full with corn, potatoes, beans, and peas. We could tell if days of hunger were approaching or not by how much was in the granary. Adjoining the courtyard was a huge kraal for cows, with smaller sheds for calves. Women collected the cow dung and goat droppings and deposited them at a dump site by the main entrance to the yard. Over the years the dump site had grown into a hill covered by green stinging nettles. The hill was so huge and it seemed to me a wonder that grown-ups were able to climb up and down it with so much ease. Sloping down from the hill was a forested landscape. As a child just beginning to walk, I used to follow, with my eyes, my mothers and the older siblings as they went past the main gate to our yard, and it seemed to me that the forest mysteriously swallowed them up in the morning, and in the evening, as mysteriously, disgorged them unharmed. It was only later when I was able to walk a bit farther from the yard that I saw that there were paths among the trees. I learned that down beyond the forest was the Limuru Township and across the railway line, white-owned plantations where my older siblings went to pick tea leaves for pay.

Then things changed, I don't know how gradually or suddenly, but they changed. The cows and the goats were the first to go, leaving behind empty sheds. The dump site was no longer the depository of cow dung and goat droppings but garbage only. Its height became less threatening in time and I too could run up and down with ease. Then our mothers stopped cultivating the fields around our courtyard; they now worked in other fields far from the compound. My father's *thingira* was abandoned, and now the women trekked some distance to take food to him. I was aware of trees being cut down, leaving only stumps, soil being dug up, followed by pyrethrum planting. It was strange to see the forest retreating as the pyrethrum fields advanced. More remarkable, my sisters and brothers were working seasonally in the new pyrethrum fields that had eaten up our forest, where before they had worked only across the rails in the European-owned tea plantations.

The changes in the physical and social landscape were not occurring in any discernible order; they merged into each other, all a little confusing. But, somehow, in time, I began to connect a few threads, and things became clearer as if I was emerging from a mist. I learned that our land was not quite our land; that our compound was part of property owned by an African landlord, Lord Reverend Stanley Kahahu, or Bwana Stanley as we called him; that we were now *ahoi*, tenants at will. How did we come to be *ahoi* on our own land? Had we lost our traditional land to Europeans? The mist had not cleared entirely.

My father, fairly aloof, talked very little about his past. Our mothers, around whom our lives revolved, seemed reluctant to divulge details of what they knew about it. However, bits and pieces, gleaned from whispers, hints, and occasional anecdotes, gradually coalesced into a narrative of his life and his side of the family.

My paternal grandfather was originally a Maasai child who strayed into a Gĩkũyũ homestead somewhere in Mũrang'a either as war ransom, a captive, or an abandoned child escaping some hardship like famine. Initially, he did not know the Gĩkũyũ language and the Maasai words he uttered frequently sounded to a Gĩkũyũ ear like *tũcũ* or *tũcũka*, so they called him Ndũcũ, meaning "the child who always said *tũcũ*." He was also given the honorific generation name Mwangi. Grandfather Ndũcũ, it is said, eventually married two wives, both named Wangeci. With one of the Wangecis he had two sons, Njinjũ, or Baba Mũkũrũ, as we called him, and my father, Thiong'o, as well as three daughters, Wanjirũ, Njeri, and Wairimũ. With the second Wangeci, he had two other boys, Kariũki and Mwangi Karuithia, also known as Mwangi the surgeon, so called because

he later became a specialist in male circumcision and practiced his profession throughout Gĩkũyũ and Maasailand.

I was not destined to meet my grandfather Ndũcũ or
grandmother Wangeci. A mysterious illness afflicted the
region. My grandfather was among the first to go, followed
quickly by his two wives and daughter Wanjirũ. Just before
dying, my grandmother, believing that the family was under
a fatal curse from the past or a strong bewitchment from
jealous neighbors—for how could people drop dead just like
that after a bout of body heat?—commanded my father and
his brother to seek refuge with relatives who had already
emigrated to Kabete, miles away, among them being their
sisters Njeri and Wairimũ. They were sworn never to return
to Mũrang'a or divulge their exact origins to their progeny
so as not to tempt their descendants to go back to claim
rights to family land and meet the same fate. The two boys
kept their promise to their mother: They fled Mũrang'a.

The mysterious illness that wiped out my grandparents
and forced my father to take flight only made sense when
years later I read stories of communal afflictions in the Old
Testament. Then I would think of my father and his brother
as part of an exodus from a plague of biblical proportion, in
search of a promised land. But when I read about Arab slave
traders, missionary explorers, and even big game hunters—
young Churchill in 1907 and Theodore Roosevelt in 1909
and a long line of others to follow—I reimagined my father
and uncle as two adventurers armed with bows and arrows
traversing the same paths, dodging these hunters, fighting
off marauding lions, narrowly escaping slithery snakes, hack-

ing their way through the wild bush of a primeval forest across valleys and ridges, till they suddenly came to a plain. There they stood in awe and fear. Before their eyes were stone buildings of various heights, paths crowded with carriages of different shapes and people of various colors from black to white. Some of the white people sat in carriages pulled and pushed by black men. These must be the white spirits, the *mizungu,* and this, the Nairobi they had heard about as having sprung from the bowels of the earth. But nothing had prepared them for the railway lines and the terrifying monster that vomited fire and occasionally made a blood-curdling cry.

Nairobi was created by that monster. Initially an assembly center for the massive material for railway construction and the extensive supporting services, Nairobi had quickly mushroomed into a town of thousands of Africans, hundreds of Asians, and a handful of cantankerous Europeans who dominated it. By 1907, when Winston Churchill, as Henry Campbell-Bannerman's parliamentary undersecretary of state for the colonies, visited nine-year-old Nairobi, he would write that every white man in the capital was "a politician and most of them are leaders of political parties," and he expressed incredulity that "a centre so new should be able to produce so many divergent and conflicting interests, or that a community so small should be able to give to each such vigorous and even vehement expression."*

The big houses in the plains affected the two brothers

---

* Winston S. Churchill, *My African Journey* (Leo Cooper, 1968), p. 18.

differently. After staying with their auntie at Uthiru, my uncle moved away from the hurly-burly of town to seek his fortune in the more rural parts of Ndeiya and Limuru, with the Karaũ family as his base. But my father, fascinated and intrigued by the urban center with its white and black dwellers, remained. Eventually he got a job as a domestic worker in a European house. Once again details about this phase of his life in a white house were few, except for the story of how he escaped induction into the First World War.

From the time of the Berlin Conference of 1885 that divided Africa into spheres of influence among European powers, the Germans and the British had been rivals for the colonization of East African territories as exemplified by two adventurers: Karl Peters, founder of the German East Africa Company in 1885; and Frederick Lugard of the Imperial British East Africa Company, incorporated in 1888 by Sir William Mackinnon. The territories that these private companies carved out for themselves with the "reluctant" backing of their respective leaders, Bismarck and Gladstone, were later nationalized, which is to say colonized. And when the mother country coughed, the colonial baby contracted full-blown flu. So when in Sarajevo, on June 28, 1914, a Serbian student, Gavrilo Princip, assassinated Franz Ferdinand, heir to the Austro-Hungarian Empire, and thus launched a European war among the emerging rival empires, the two colonial states, Tanganyika and Kenya, fought on the side of their mothers, hence against each other; the German forces, led by General von Lettow-Vorbeck, were pitted against the British, led by General Jan Smuts. But it was not just the European colonists fighting one another—after all, they made up less than 1 percent of the population. They drafted many Africans as soldiers and members of the Carrier Corps. The African soldiers died, in combat and from disease and other ills, out of all proportion to the European soldiers. Their participation would be all but forgotten except for the fact that the places where they camped, in Nairobi and Dar es Salaam, would bear the name Kariokoo, a Swahilinized form of Carrier Corps. Since the Africans were being forced into a war whose origins and causes the natives knew nothing about, many like my father did whatever they could to avoid the draft. Every time he knew he was going for a medical exam, he would chew leaves of a certain plant that raised his temperature to an alarming level. But there are other versions of the story suggesting the connivance of his white employer, who did not want to lose my father's domestic services.

From this historical event, and my father's age group, Nyarĩgĩ, I was able to calculate that he was born sometime between 1890 and 1896, the years that Queen Victoria, through her prime minister, Robert Cecil, 3rd Marquess of Salisbury, took over what was then a company "property" and called it East Africa Protectorate, and, in 1920, Kenya colony and protectorate. Immediate proof of effective British ownership was the creation of the Uganda railway from Kilindini, Mombasa—the highway of the monster that my father saw spitting out fire even as it roared.

The Nairobi where my father now worked was a product of that change in formal ownership and the completion of the railway line that eased the traffic of white settlers into the interior from 1902 onward. After the First World War, which ended with the Treaty of Versailles of June 1919, white ex-soldiers were rewarded with African lands, some of the land belonging to surviving African soldiers, accelerating dispossession, forced labor, and tenancy-at-will on lands now owned by settlers, such tenants otherwise known as squatters. In exchange for the use of the land, the squatters provided cheap labor and sold their harvests to the white landlord at a price determined by him. The buttressed white settlerdom did meet resistance from Africans, the most significant movement at the time being the East African Association, founded in 1921, the first countrywide African political organization, and led by Harry Thuku, who captured the imagination of all working Africans, including my father. In him, an African working class, the new social force on the stage of Kenyan history, and of which my father was now part, had found its voice. Thuku forged connections with Marcus Garvey's international black nationalism to the West, in America, and with Gandhi's Indian nationalism to the East, the latter through his alliance with Manilal A. Desai, a leader of local Indians. His activities were closely monitored by the colonial secret police and discussed in the London colonial office as a menace to white power. Both Gandhi and Thuku had called for civil disobedience at about the same time in their respective countries. To suppress this Kenyan link between Gandhian nationalism and Garveyite black nationalism, the British arrested Thuku in March 1922 and deported him to Kismayu, now in Somalia, where he languished for seven years. It is probably a coincidence, but an interesting one all the same, that Gandhi was arrested on March 10, barely a few days after Thuku. The workers reacted to news of Thuku's arrest with a mass protest outside the Central Police Station in Nairobi. Aided by settlers who were drinking beer and liquor on the terraces of the Norfolk Hotel, the police shot dead 150 protesters including one of the women's leaders, Nyanjirũ Mũthoni. I don't know if my father was present at the mass protest and mass murder, but he certainly would have been affected by the subsequent call for a general strike by domestic workers, upon whose labor the white aristocracy depended entirely. My father fled Nairobi altogether, avoiding the emerging political turmoil in the same way he had escaped the plague, the way he had evaded the draft during the First World War. He followed his brother to the rural safety of Limuru.

But Nairobi had left its mark on him. From his European employer my father had learned a few choice English words and phrases—"bloody fool," "nigger," and "bugger"—but which he Gĩkũyũnized as *mburaribuu, kaniga gaka, mbaga ĩno,* and which he used freely to address any of his children at whom he was angry. From his employment he had saved enough money to buy some goats and cows that in time had bred more goats and cows, and by the time he fled the capital, he already had a reasonable herd that his brother helped look after. Eventually my father bought land in Limuru from Njamba Kĩbũkũ. He paid in goats under the traditional system of oral agreement in the presence of witnesses. Later, Njamba sold the same land to Lord Stanley Kahahu, one of the early Christian converts and graduates of the Church of Scotland Mission at Kikuyu, and to his brother Edward Matumbĩ, who had made money in Molo through logging, sawing timber, and making roofing shingles for European customers. The resale was recorded under the colonial legal system, with witnesses and signed written documents. Did the religious Kahahu know that Njamba was selling the land twice, first in goats to my father and second in cash to him? Whatever his knowledge, the double transaction created a lasting tension between the two claimants, my father and Kahahu.

The hearing to determine the real owner, an on-and-off affair, at the Native Tribunal Court at Cura, dragged on for many years, but at every hearing it was a case of the legal written word against oral testimony. Orality and tradition lost to literacy and modernity. A title deed no matter how it was gotten trumped oral deeds. Kahahu emerged the rightful owner; my father retained a noninheritable right of life occupancy on the compound where he had built the five huts. The victor immediately asserted his rights by denying my father access to grazing and cultivation on the rest of the land.

Did my father ever reflect on the irony that he had lost out to a black landlord, a product of the white missionary center at Kikuyu, under the same legal system that had created White Highlands out of the African-owned highlands? He had more immediate things to worry about than the ironies of history: how to feed his children and the vast herd of goats and cows.

My maternal grandfather, Ngũgĩ wa Gĩkonyo, helped my father out. He gave him grazing and cultivation rights on the lands he owned, lands that stretched to the Indian shops, the African shops, and beyond, on the African side of the rails. My father's new *thingira* and cattle kraal were located between the edge of a forest of blue gum and eucalyptus trees that Grandfather Ngũgĩ owned and the outskirts of the African market.* My father's wives and children remained at the old homestead.

So, despite the legal blow and its consequences, my father's reputation as the richest in cows and goats continued, as well as his reputation for having a disciplined home and an eye for beautiful women going all the way back to when he won his first bride.

---

* The forest no longer exists. It is now the site of the extended Limuru Township, after the original Indian shops were moved from the old site.

Wangarĩ's looks and character had been the talk across hills and valleys, between Limuru and Riũki. Actually the two regions were near each other, but in those days when there was no transport they seemed many miles apart. Uncle Njinjũ, my father's brother, was the first to be smitten by her looks and vowed to get her as his second wife. It is not known how Uncle Njinjũ, or Baba Mũkũrũ as we called him, first heard of her or came into contact with her or her family. It is not even known whether he had actually met her. Most likely he had simply set in motion one of those family-to-family wooings mediated by third parties. Property, in cows and goats, and good character were more persuasive than looks, and, presumably, the two orphans who had started with nothing but had brought themselves up to match the achievements of the young men of their age, in wealth in goats, had demonstrated they did not rely on their handsome looks but on their hands and minds.

Since their flight from Mũrang'a, my father and Baba Mũkũrũ had traveled slightly different paths and developed different attitudes to life. My father had acquired urban airs in dress and outlook; for instance, he had a cavalier attitude to traditional rites and practices. My uncle on the other hand had made his way through rural cultivation and herding, observing traditional values and rites, like those performed in his marriage to his first wife. Still, the fact that Baba Mũkũrũ was now aiming for a second bride, while my father was still unmarried, was a measure of my uncle's success and validated the choice he had made to avoid the city in favor of the countryside.

Accompanied by my father, Baba Mũkũrũ took a delegation that included nonfamily spokesmen, for one never talked on his own behalf in such matters, and they went to Wangarĩ's father, Ikĩgu. Everything went well, the drinks, the formal preliminaries, until the bride was called in to meet her suitor. They should have better prepared her because, on entering, her eyes fell on the younger of the two men, my father. Corrections afterward about the real suitor fell on the deaf ears of a young woman being asked to choose between being the second wife of an older man or the first wife of another who exuded both youth and modernity.

By the time they returned home, the fortunes of the two brothers had changed; Wangarĩ had fallen in love with the young urbanite, my father, and eventually became his first wife. The brotherly relationship, though not broken, became strained, and remained so for life. Love had come between the two men who in their youth had depended on each other in their quest for a new life far from home.

I don't know how my father later obtained his second

wife, Gacoki. Rumors hinted that his first wife, Wangarĩ, needing extra hands in managing their growing wealth in cows and goats, had helped attract Gacoki to the home. More likely, news of the poetry of the heart and the rhythm of work between Wangarĩ and my father may have allured Gacoki, the beautiful daughter of Gĩthieya, long before my father actually proposed. The experience of my own mother, the third wife, provides some evidence of my father's ways of wooing.

My mother, Wanjikũ, was of few words. But those words carried the authority of the silence that preceded their utterance. Now and then, words would gush from her mouth, opening a little window into her soul. I once asked her, during one of those moments of well-being that follow a good steaming meal, Why did you consent to polygamy? Why did you accept being the third wife of my father, who already had older children—Wangeci and Tumbo with Wangarĩ, and Gĩtundu with Gacoki?

It was because of his two first wives, Wangarĩ and Gacoki, and their children, she said with light and shadows from the wood fire playing on her face. They were always together, such harmony, and I often wondered how it would feel to be in their company. And your father? He was not to be denied. I don't know how he knew where I worked in my father's fields, well, your grandfather's, but he would somehow appear, just smile and say a few words. What a pity if such a hardworking beauty should ever team up with a lazy man, he would tease me. Those were no small words coming from a man who had so many goats and cows, and he had acquired all that wealth by his own toil. But I did not want him to think that I would simply fall for his words and reputation, and I challenged him. How do I know that you are not one of those who work their wives to death and then claim the wealth came from his hands alone? The following day he came back, a hoe on his shoulder. As if to prove that he did not include himself among the lazy, without waiting for my invitation even, he started to work. It became a playful but serious competition to see who would tire first. I held my own, she said with a touch of pride in her prowess. The only break was when I lit a fire and roasted some potatoes. Don't you think you and I should combine our strengths in a home? he again asked. I said: Just because of one day's work on a field already broken? Another day, he found me trying to clear some bush to expand my farm. He joined in the clearing and by the end of the day we were both exhausted but neither of us would admit to it. He went away and I thought that he would never appear again. But he did come back, on another day, without a hoe, an enigma of a smile on his face. Oh, yes, such a day it was! The crop was in bloom, the entire field covered with pea flowers of different colors. I always remember the butterflies, so many; and I was not afraid of the bees that competed with the butterflies. He took out a bead necklace and said: Will you wear this for me? Well, I did not say yes or no, but I took it and wore it, she said with an audible sigh.

My mother would not answer follow-up questions, but

what she had said was enough to tell me how she became the third of my father's wives, but not sufficient to tell me how she came to lose her place, as the youngest and latest, to Njeri, the fourth wife, or even how she felt about the new addition to the family.

I was born into an already functioning community of wives, grown-up brothers, sisters, children about my age, and a single patriarch, and into settled conventions about how we acknowledged our relation to one another. But it could be confusing and I had to grow into the system. The women themselves would never refer to each other by their names; to each other, they were always the daughter of their respective fathers: Mwarĩ wa Ikĩgu for Wangarĩ, Mwarĩ wa Gĩthieya for Gacoki, Mwarĩ wa Ngũgĩ for Wanjikũ, and Mwarĩ wa Kabicũria for Njeri, the youngest. I came to learn that when talking about them to a third party, the first wife, Wangarĩ, was my elder mother, *maitũ mũkũrũ*, and the other two were each my younger mother, *maitũ mũnyinyi*. The unqualified *maitũ* was reserved for my biological mother. Otherwise, it was always Yes, Mother, or Thank you, Mother, when addressing each woman directly. But one could also distinguish among them by referring to them as mother of any one of their own biological children. My half siblings could call my mother "Ngũgĩ's mother" when talking about her to a third person.

It would be a bit more complicated when talking about

several siblings to an outsider. Our naming was informed by a symbolic system of reincarnation that meant that each mother had children alternatively named after her side of the family and my father's side, and hence many of the children had identical names to those that came from my father's line. There was the broad category of brothers and sisters from the same mother and half sisters and half brothers when introducing them to a third person. Otherwise we were differentiated from one another by our biological mother; for instance, I was always Ngũgĩ wa Wanjikũ. In addition, many of my sisters and brothers had nicknames they had given themselves or had been given by others, and these were individual to them. There was Gacungwa, "Little Orange"; Gatunda, "Little Fruit"; Kahabu, "Half-a-Cent"; Kĩbirũri, "the Player of Spinning Tops"; Wabia, "Rupee"; Mbecai, "Money"; Ngiree, "Gray"; Gũthera, "Miss Clean"; Tumbo, "Big Tummy." I grew up knowing them by these, and it was a shock when later I learned their real names, which seemed less real. I came to accept that within the framework of Thiong'o's family, there were multiple ways of identifying oneself or being identified by others.

The four women forged a strong alliance vis-à-vis the outside world, their husband, and even their children. Any of them could rebuke and discipline any one of us kids, the culprit likely to get additional punishment if she complained to the biological mother. We could feed from any of the mothers. They resolved serious tensions through discussion, one of them, usually the eldest, acting as the arbiter.

There were also subtle, shifting alliances among them, but these were kept in check by their general solidarity as my father's brides. They had their own individuality. Njeri, the youngest, was strong-framed with a sharp, irreverent tongue. She brooked no nonsense from anyone. She was known to speak on behalf of any of the other women against an outsider even if it was a man. She could openly defy my father but she also knew when and how to back off. She was the undeclared defense minister of the homestead. My mother was a thinker and good listener loved for her generosity and respected for her legendary capacity for work. Though she would not confront my father openly, she was stubborn and let her actions speak for her. She was like the minister of works. Gacoki, shy and kind, disliked conflicts, adopting a live-and-let-live attitude even when she was the wronged party. She, the minister of peace, was the most scared of my father. Wangarĩ, the eldest, was always calm as if she had seen it all. Her power over my father was through a look, a word, or a gesture of disapproval, as if reminding him that she was the one who had chosen him over his brother. She was the minister of culture, a philosopher who drew from experience and cited proverbs to make a point.

She was a great storyteller. Every evening we children gathered around the fireside in her hut, and the performance would begin. Sometimes, particularly on weekends, the older siblings would bring their friends and it would then become a storytelling session for all. One told a story. After it ended, another person from the audience would say something like, "That reminds me of . . . ," or such other words, a signal that he or she was going to tell a story, even if, as it turned out in most cases, the new story had nothing to do with the one that apparently provoked it. But the comment did not always mean another story. It could also bring a narration of an episode illustrating the truth of an aspect of the story. Sometimes such opinions and illustrations generated heated debates that had no clear winner, and they often flowed into yet other stories. Or sometimes they led to stories about events in the land and the world. Like when they talked about age groups and how times change, citing the case of Harry Thuku, whose political fire of the 1920s had become cold ash following his release in 1929 after seven years of exile. The society of three letters (Kĩama kĩa Ndemwa Ithatũ), as the Kikuyu Central Association (KCA), the successor to Harry Thuku's East African Association, was called after it was also banned by the colonial state in 1941, was very angry with the new Thuku, who talked of persuasion and putting out fires in place of demands backed by threats of fire. The arguments about the merits and demerits of the two approaches were above my head and quite boring, but the historical anecdotes were all right because for me they were still part of the oral universe of storytelling. Some of them sounded stranger than fiction: like the case of a white man called Hitler refusing to shake the hand of the fastest runner in the world in 1936 because the man, Jesse Owens, was black.

I looked forward to these evenings; it seemed to me a glorious wonder that such beautiful and sometimes scary stories could issue from their mouths. Best for me were those stories in which the audience would join in the singing of the chorus. The melody was invariably captivating; it felt like I had been transported to another world of endless harmony even in sadness. This intensified my anticipation of what would happen next. I hated it when some members would interrupt the storyteller to dispute the accuracy of a sequence. Why not wait for their turn? I was keen to hear what happened next even when I already knew the story.

Sometimes the sessions would move to the other women's huts, but the festive air would not be as intense. Gacoki and Njeri were not good storytellers and hardly contributed. My mother was also not good at it, but when pressed she fell back on either of the two stories she always told. One was about a blacksmith who goes to a smithy far away and leaves his wife pregnant. An ogre helps her deliver, but when it comes to nursing he eats up all the food and drinks up all the porridge intended for the mother. In exchange for castor oil seeds, a pigeon agrees to deliver a message to the blacksmith, who comes back and kills the ogre and is happily reunited with his wife and family. Another was a simple, almost plotless tale about a man with an incurable wound who does not give up but embarks on a quest for a cure. He does not know the dwelling place of the famous medicine man; he only knows him by the name of Ndiro. In asking strangers for the way, he describes the medicine man in terms of his gait, dance steps, and the rhythmic jingles around his ankles that sound his name, Ndiro. This story was popular with us children. We could visualize the medicine man and would join in the chorus, sometimes stepping on the ground and calling out "Ndiro" in unison. One of my half sisters liked the tale so much that she adopted it as her own whenever it was her turn to tell a story.

In the daytime, we would try to retell the stories we had heard among ourselves, but they did not come out as powerfully as when told around the fireside, the entire space jammed with eager participatory listeners. Daylight, our mothers always told us, drove stories away, and it seemed true.

There was one exception that defied the rules of day and night. Wabia was the fifth child, or the second daughter, of Wangarĩ's seven children, four of whom had physical challenges of one kind or other, the severest being those of two siblings: Gĩtogo and Wabia. Gĩtogo had lost his power of speech on the same day that his sister Wabia lost the power of sight and motion. The two were born with sight and hearing, but one day when Wabia was carrying her baby brother Gĩtogo on her back, lightning had struck. Wabia complained that somebody had put out the sun; and Gĩtogo, with gestures, that the same person had stopped all sound. Later, he learned to speak in signs accompanied by undecipherable guttural sounds. Gĩtogo, handsome and strongly built, had no other physical challenges. But Wabia had lost all power in the leg joints. She could stand up or take steps only with the aid of two walking sticks.

She always sat or lay down in the courtyard, under the roof of her mother's hut. Sometimes she took a few steps and then lay out in the sun. But curiously her voice and memory came to be more powerful. When she sang, which she did often, her voice could be heard far away. She had never been to church, but through listening to those who had been she remembered what she had heard sung by others; in time she became a storehouse of lyrics and melodies sung in different churches. But she also knew many other songs, particularly those in stories she had heard at her mother's fireside. For her, the story did not flee in daytime, and we, the children, became the grateful recipients of her powers of retention. In the evening she never contributed to the storytelling, she just listened, but on the following day she could retell the same stories with an imaginative power that made them even more interesting and delightful than in their first telling. Through the modulation of her voice, she would create anew their poetry and drama. She owned the stories. Of course we had to be nice to her, love one another, and obey our parents for her to release the story in daytime. If we quarreled among ourselves or disobeyed our mothers, she claimed that the story had run away in sorrow. We had to coax and promise her that we would be on good behavior. Some of the kids would demand stories from her and when she refused would take away her walking sticks, in vengeance. But she never would give in to their demands. I was one of the most obedient, to her at least, and would bring her water or retrieve her walking sticks. She also liked it that I was one of the most persistent seekers of her performance. More than her mother or other narrators, Wabia was possessed of imaginative power that took me to worlds unknown, worlds that I was later able to glimpse only through reading fiction. Whenever I think of that phase of my childhood, it is in terms of the stories at Wangarĩ's hut at night and their rebirth in her daughter's voice in daytime.

Though I did not know it at the time, it would be two of Wangarĩ's other children who would connect me to a history unfolding in the colonial state and in the world. First was the eldest male in my father's household, Tumbo, an odd nickname because he had no visibly big belly. He had no visible job either, but it was whispered that he was a *gĩcerũ*. There were people answering to the name Gĩcerũ, but this could refer to the fact that they were light-skinned. For them it was simply a name and not a job. How could one have a profession called "white"? It was only later, when I learned that the word, as used, was derived from the Swahili word *kacheru*, which means "informer," that I knew that he worked in low-level undercover police intelligence.

Her third son, Joseph Kabae, was also a mystery, emerging in my mind as an image in a mist. Since I had not met him in person, the outline was formed through hints and odd bits only. As a boy, grazing our father's herd, he had gotten into a fight with a bigger boy, a bully who always came upon him when he was milking my father's cows. The bully would drink some of the milk by force and Kabae would get into trouble. One day in anger and self-defense, Kabae fatally stabbed the boy with a knife. He was arrested, but being under age he was taken to Wamũnyũ, a reform trade school, where he got some formal education. After this—I don't know if it was voluntary or forced—he went to fight for King George VI, in the Second World War, as a member of the King's African Rifles.

The KAR, as it was known, was formed in 1902, an outgrowth of two earlier units, the East African Rifles and the Central African Regiment, the brainchild of Captain Lugard. He was famous as the author of the British Indirect Rule, the strategy of using the natives of one region to fight the natives of another region, and in each community, to use the chiefs, traditional or created, to suppress their own people on behalf of the British Crown. The regiment had earlier played a big role in the pursuit of the elusive German von Lettow-Vorbeck in the First World War and against the Ashanti king, the Asantahene, in the Ashanti wars. The men of the regiment sang of themselves as king's men marching to his orders.

Twafunga safari
Twafunga safari
Amri ya nani?
Ya Bwana,
Tufunge safari.

We are marching on
We are marching on
At whose order?
The king's orders
Let's march on.

Kabae was not the only one from our extended family who fought in the Second World War. Cousin Mwangi, the eldest son of Baba Mũkũrũ, had joined. Names of strange people—Mussolini, Hitler, Franco, Stalin, Churchill, and

Roosevelt—and places—America, Germany, Italy, and Russia, Japan, Madagascar, and Burma—occasionally cropped up in the story sessions at Wangarĩ's fireside. These names and places were vague in outline, and, like those surrounding Harry Thuku earlier, were really shadows in a mist. Was this Hitler, for instance, the same who had refused to shake hands with Jesse Owens? I could understand them only in terms of scary ogres versus heroes in the never-never land of orality. Hitler and Mussolini, who threatened to enslave Africans, were the bad, ugly ogres, the proof of their evil intent being next door. Even before I was born, Benito Mussolini had entered Ethiopia in 1936 and had forced the African emperor Haile Selassie into exile and added insult to injury by creating Italian East Africa out of Ethiopia and neighboring territories. Us today; you tomorrow, Haile Selassie had told the League of Nations, who had watched the invasion of Ethiopia, a member state, with silence. Folk talked about these episodes as if they were part of their everyday life. How did these young men and women, some of them just workers in the nearby Limuru Bata Shoe Company, know such stories and the goings-on in times past and places far away? The young dancers who sang of the bad Hitler marching down to Kenya to put yokes around African people's necks reinforced the image of a dread beast let loose in the world. But pitted against this beast and its deadly intentions were brave characters, part of the British army of saviors, and among them were Cousin Mwangi and Brother Kabae. We heard of their exploits in Abyssinia in the campaign against Mussolini's Italian East Africa, and a lot of

new names of places, such as Addis Ababa, Eritrea, Moga-
dishu, Italian and British Somaliland, entered the conversation. Of course the complexities of warfare eluded me. Bits
and pieces of stories coalesced into whispers of Mussolini's
soldiers' surrender. To me it was quite simple. Heroes had
defeated ogres, at least those marching toward us, and our
brother and our cousin had played a part in the victory. In
my mind, Joseph Kabae, whom I had not met, was the most
heroic and Mussolini's soldiers had really surrendered to
him. He and I were connected by blood, our father's blood,
but he was still a character in a fairyland far away.

But evidence of war was not to be found simply in stories;
it was all around us. Peasant farmers could sell their food
only through the government marketing board. Movement
of food across regions was not permitted without a license,
creating shortages and famine in some areas. Though I did
not know the reasons at the time, this system of food production and distribution was actually the colony's contribution to the British war economy. In Limuru, the prohibition
produced a famous smuggler, Karugo, who drove his truck
so fast that he often eluded the pursuing police. He was
finally arrested and jailed, but he became a legend in the
popular imagination, giving rise to the expression "Karugo's
speedometer." *Tura na cia Karugo* meant "speed away," or
"don't worry about any speed limit."

There was also the visual evidence in the soldiers that
passed through Limuru, who at times would get stuck in the
country dirt tracks that passed for roads. To make the tracks
more passable, the government turned them into wider mur-

ram roads. In digging up the murram, the government works left a deep rectangular quarry the size of a soccer field near the Manguo marshes around Kimunya's corner, just below the Kahahu estate. With the improvement, the soldiers would sometimes stop and park their vehicles by the roadside and have their lunches in any open space in the forest bushes around. They would give cookies and canned meat to herd boys. One of my half brothers, Njinjũ wa Njeri, then the main assistant herd boy to my father, would often bring some home, and talk about the military, but he never mentioned having seen our Joseph Kabae among them. Did he, wherever he was, also park vehicles by the roadside and eat cookies and canned meat and give some to herd boys?

One day, two of a convoy of trucks full of military men fell off the road into the cavernous murram quarry. The rest of the convoy stopped and parked by the roadside. There was mayhem of movement among the rescuers and the rescued. News spread quickly. Practically the whole village was there to see the wounded and the dead being carried away. The sounds of mourning were terrible, especially for us children. But worse for the Thiong'o family was the rumor that began to circulate that Kabae may have been part of the military convoy. There was nobody to ask. Stories of his having been far away in Abyssinia did not allay our concerns. The silence of the government exacerbated our fears. I felt deprived of a war hero, a half brother I would now never see.

But one night he came home in an army truck, two headlights splitting the darkness. There was not much of a road to our homestead. The truck simply made two tracks past

Lord Kahahu's orchard to our compound. Unfortunately, it had been raining. The truck got stuck in the mud, and as the driver tried to rev it out, the truck hit my mother's hut and dug deeper in the mud. The army men in green khaki fatigues and army hats spent most of their night visit trying to dig it out using flashlights to see. We crowded around them, and I could not even make out who Kabae was except when he, a shadowy figure among shadowy figures, left his men digging and said hurried greetings to the family. He was back from the East African Campaign, resting and recharging in Nairobi, before redeployment to other fronts in Madagascar or even Burma. Apparently he and his friends had taken the truck without permission, hoping to be away for only a few hours, long enough for Kabae to quench, a little, the thirst for home that he must have felt in his years away. It was also an opportunity for him and his non-Gĩkũyũ comrades-in-arms, who must have felt even farther from home, to eat a home-cooked meal as opposed to their rations of cookies and canned meat. He mentioned some of the countries of their origin—Uganda, Tanganyika, and Nyasaland. The King's African Rifles had people from all over Africa, he said. By the time they dug out the truck, they could only eat hurriedly and were anxious to leave and return to camp in Nairobi. So we did not spend much time with him, but I hardly slept thinking of the drama that had just ended. It was as if Kabae had jumped out of a story, said a hello, a good-bye, and then jumped back into the story. Hitting my mother's hut and digging out the truck at night was not exactly the most heroic homecoming for one who had been all over the world fighting ogres, but then his was the first motor vehicle ever to come to our homestead. We realized how big our brother was when the landlord did not raise any complaints about the tracks the truck had made through his land or about the bent orchard trees. The visit was forever engraved in my mind and talks of the big war now brought back memories of a military truck stuck in the mud by my mother's hut.

I don't know how long it was after Kabae's visit, but more magical happenings followed. A white man came to our homestead. Although white people owned the tea planta-tions on the other side of the railway, and I had even heard that there were white owners of the Limuru Bata Shoe fac-tory, the nearest thing to a white man I had seen at close quarters were the Indian shopkeepers. But here was a real white man, on foot, in our homestead, and we ran by his side calling out, *Mũthũngũ, mũthũngũ.* He said something like *bono* or *buena* and then asked for eggs. My mother gave him some, even refusing his money in exchange, and he uttered something like *grazie* and went away saying *ciao,* which we took for yet another word for "thank you." We followed behind him, a crowd of children, still calling out *Mũthũngũ.* And then came the shock.

We saw white men making a road, white men who were not supervising blacks but were actually breaking the stones themselves. Later more of these workmen came to our place asking for eggs, *mayai,* throwing words out like *buonasera, buongiorno, pronto, grazie,* but the word that was most fre-quent and common to all of them, the one that lingered in the mind, was *bono*. We nicknamed them Bono: I would learn that they were Italian prisoners of war taken between May and November 1941 when the Italians surrendered at Amba Alage and Gondar, ending the East African Campaign. The prisoners were imported labor, charged with building the road from Nairobi to the interior, parallel to the railway line that was first built by imported Indian labor. The prisoners became a regular sight in our village, and every house had an Italian tale to tell.

Ours concerned Wabia, Kabae's sister, who could not take a step let alone walk without the aid of two walking sticks. After many months, it could even have been a year, the first Bono visitor came back to our homestead. This time, after collecting his eggs and a chicken for which he paid, his attention was attracted to Wabia, and in his halting Swahili he asked many questions about her. I cannot recall what words he actually uttered, but one of my half brothers claimed that he said that he could bring her some medicine that could cure her. I loved Wabia. It would be wonderful if she could get back the gift of sight and the power of walking without support. It would mean that white people's medicine was more magical than anything we could ever imagine, even in the stories that Wabia told so well.

We waited for the Italian. He became the white Ndiro of our imagination, the medicine man in the story my mother told, except that he had an Italian accent, and we were not looking for his dwelling place; he was coming to us, and we were simply waiting for his return. The road was now past Limuru and the Bonos did not haunt our area as regularly as they used to do, but we did not lose hope: The Italian would surely bring a cure. What a welcome it would be for Kabae to come back from the war and be welcomed home by a sister with all her powers of walking and sight restored!

Images of Kabae's visit, despite being blurred by time and, now, overtaken by our new expectations, would not go away, and sometimes they came back with the full weight of their unreality whenever the subject of the war reappeared in conversation or in performance. Most popular was *mũthuũ*, a boys' call-and-response dance in which, among other verses, the soloist-narrator, who had never left the village, boasts of many heroic deeds including fighting in the jungles of Burma, and finally returning home having dropped bombs in Japan and routed Hitler and Hirohito. These fictional accomplishments were reasons that the heroic soloist should be feared and obeyed by his chorus. Indeed, the lead singer-dancer looked ferocious as he suddenly whipped out a wooden sword that had been tied around his waist, twirled it in his hands, then threw it in the air, catching it deftly while keeping in step with the dance. Burma, bombs, Hirohito, new words were added to my ever-increasing vocabulary of the war. But we still waited for the Italian.

A time came when I no longer saw the Bono Mayai in any of our villages walking about or asking for anything. They did not come back. Our white Ndiro did not return. Wabia, my dear half sister, was never cured. But the Bonos left their architectural mark in the church they had built by the road on the edge of the Rift Valley in their hours of rest; and their sociobiological mark in broken families and fatherless brown babies born in several of the villages they had visited.

And then our half brother came home finally. It was 1945; the war was over, the soldiers demobilized. There were tears and laughter. Cousin Mwangi, first son of Baba Mũkũrũ, had been killed in action; nobody could tell us where, but Palestine, the Middle East, and even Burma were variously mentioned. But Kabae had survived, a legend, big to us, bigger and even more educated than the sons of Lord Reverend Stanley Kahahu. There were even whispers of a dalliance with one of the daughters of the landlord.

Kabae, the ex-soldier, became a ladies' man, a chain-smoker, and partial to beer, which he bought from Indian-owned licensed liquor stores but drank off premises, on the grass just outside the backyard; he was one of the few Africans who could afford bottle after bottle of beer made by the European-owned East African Breweries. Later an African shop owner, Athabu Muturi, was allowed to sell the European beer at the Limuru marketplace, and the drinking shifted to the backyard of his store.

I was disappointed that Kabae rarely came home, and when he did he hardly ever talked in depth and elaborate detail about the big war, at least when I was present. He did not even talk about Cousin Mwangi, whether they had met or not, during the war. Once he mentioned Madagascar, but briefly, as if he had only made a stop there. Another time he commented on the *mũthuũ* dancers and their reference to Burma and Japan. "The jungles of Burma proved to be death traps for us in the East African Division," he said.* "Monsoon rains turned the dirt roads into rivers of mud. And the Japanese were fierce fighters. But we from East Africa proved ourselves as jungle fighters. As for the bombing of Hiroshima, well, I wasn't there. And it should not be a subject of dances. The world will never know what and how much we the Africans gave to this war." That was all, his most detailed reflection on the war. I would have liked to hear about the battles he had fought; whether he had met Mussolini and Hitler face-to-face before their surrender or shaken hands with Churchill and the Russian generals.

In one of the rare times that he came home, the visit coincided with a storytelling session at his mother's. The war and its aftermath were becoming a thing of the past. That night the topic of general discussion was languages and the habit of talking behind people's backs. It was then that Kabae chimed in reflectively on the dangers of backbiting others. He then told his story.

Once, before demobilization, he worked in an office next to that of a European woman. His friends from the army used to visit him and they talked in Gĩkũyũ about the woman, wondering what it would be like to sleep with her, but sometimes teasing him that he had probably done it already. He himself chose not to respond and cautioned them against such talk. In Kenya in those days it was illegal for an African male to have a dalliance with a European

* A reference to the Eleventh East African Division, part of the Fourteenth Army under General Bill Slim. The hills along the Kabaw Valley were known as Death Valley.

woman. But it was also because he genuinely felt uneasy about small talk about a person who was present but, it was assumed, could not follow what was being said about her.

One day when they were engrossed in such talk, the woman happened to pass by. She greeted them in perfect Gĩkũyũ, adding that in her view, every woman, black or white, had the same anatomy. The men literally flew through whatever opening they could easily access, never to be seen anywhere near that building. Thank you, she said, turning to Kabae.

After demobilization Kabae set up his own secretarial and legal services in the African shopping center in Limuru. He was reputed to be one of the fastest typists on a Remington typewriter; the rapidity and volume of the raucous noise could be heard from the streets, attracting attention. People lined up outside his office for legal advice and to have him write letters for them in English. His became an all-purpose information center in matters of colonial bureaucracy. This enhanced Kabae's reputation as among the most learned in the area. For us, the Thiong'o family, he was by far the best educated. This may have sparked my desire for learning, which I kept to myself. Why should I voice desires impossible to fulfill?

As a child, I wanted to be with my mother all the time. If she went anywhere without me, I would cry for many hours. It earned me the nickname Kĩrĩri, "Crybaby," because no lullabies or admonitions from others would stop me. I would cry myself to sleep, and somehow by the time I woke up my mother would be around. Conveniently forgetting the few times I woke up and she was not there, which meant more crying and more sleeping and waking up, I assumed that my crying had had something to do with her reappearance.

I must have slept, at one time, so long that when I woke up I found my mother holding a baby in her hands. I remember being outdone in my crying by this baby who would not leave my dear mother's breasts or back or hands. His cries had more power than mine because my mother would stop everything and attend to him. My crying ended when I was told that my mother had been to some place to get me the baby so that I could have a younger brother for a playmate. We were one year apart. He was named Njinjũ, after Baba Mũkũrũ, and despite sibling rivalry we later became inseparable, especially after I taught him to walk, or so I assumed because there came a time when he would imitate me in everything. My crying had really been a call for a younger playmate. My mother, almost by magic, had divined and acted on my teary desire. This belief in her magical capacity to anticipate my needs was later buttressed by her other deeds.

My eyes used to trouble me as a child. My eyelids swelled, my eyes ran. I cried a lot with pain. My mother used to take me to a traditional healer, at Kamĩri's place near Manguo's only tap water center. The healer would make small razor blade incisions along the eyebrows above the swollen eyelids. He would bleed them and then rub some medicine on the cuts, and somehow I would feel better. But this well-being would last only a few weeks. I was in and out of the healer's shrine. I used to squint the better to see, and people teased me and called me Gacici, the little one who can barely see. I did not like it, because nicknames, even those that originated in a passing negative habit, sometimes stuck. I had succeeded in outgrowing Crybaby; I did not want it replaced by Squinting Baby.

Lord Reverend Stanley Kahahũ came to my rescue. I don't know if it was my mother who approached him or the other way around. But one day my mother bathed me and took me to the road, just outside the gates of Kahahu's house, where the reverend picked us up in his car, an old Ford Model T. I had never been inside any motor vehicle before, and I wished that my eyes didn't hurt so that I could enjoy the ride to King George VI Hospital, Nairobi, previously known as Native Civil Hospital, but now named after the king for whom my half brother Kabae had gone to war. It was the first time for my mother and me in the big city. Several looks at my eyes and the doctor said I had to be admitted. I don't know if this was necessitated by the eye condition or the fact that there were no pharmacies, that certain medicine was available only at the hospital. I was left alone in a hospital bed alongside other patients, the first time that my mother had ever left me among complete strangers. Everything including the smell was so different from the fresh-air environment at home. But somehow I managed to adjust. The other patients were kind. The doctors were kind. The togetherness of people in times of sorrow was touching.

My mother and Reverend Kahahu came to see me once. Then they left me there with a promise to return soon. I don't know how long I stayed in the hospital, two weeks, three weeks, or a month, but it felt like a long time, a long way from home. The better I felt, the more I missed my mother and home. Eventually I was discharged but I could not leave the hospital premises. I had nowhere to go, and I did not know when Lord Reverend Kahahu and my mother would come for me. I was tired of the hospital but I had no means of contacting my mother. So I did what we the children believed would effect contact with the spirit of an absent loved one. If you whispered in the mouth of a clay pot the name of a loved one, he or she would hear you. There was no clay pot around. So I took whatever looked like a pot, a jug, and whispered my mother's name. I could not believe it when soon after, the next day or so I took it, my mother turned up. I was so happy to see her without pain in my eyes. But why had she not been to see me? And why was she alone?

She explained that Reverend Kahahu had been very busy and kept on postponing the day of another visit. Eventually she could not bear it. She took the matter in her own hands, asked people how and where to catch a bus for King George, and she came for me. I was happy to be leaving for home, but I felt sad for those I was leaving behind.

We went to the bus stop. Bus service was very poor and unpredictable in those days. But eventually a bus arrived and we got in and took our seats. This time I could look through the window and see the scenes on each side of the road. It was amazing. It looked to me as if the trees and the grass were moving backward as the bus moved forward. The faster it ran forward, the faster the scenery moved backward. We drove for quite a distance. Then the conductor came to collect the fare. My mother gave him all the money she had and told him that we were going to get off at the last stop in Limuru. He looked at us strangely and then said: Mother, you are going in the wrong direction, toward Ngong, not Limuru. At the next stop, he told us to get off and wait on the other side of the road for the bus going back.

Fortunately, at that moment, a bus moving in the opposite direction came. He hailed it and spoke to the driver and the conductor. He gave my mother the money he had taken from her. The new conductor in the new bus took us back through the city and eventually dropped us at a stop, again without charging us, and we took the next bus to Limuru and home.

I was excited that I had been to the big city. I had never seen many stone buildings together. Were these the same buildings that my father had seen as a youth in flight from

Mũrang'a? Or the same that had housed half brother Kabae, the king's man? Could any of these buildings be the place where the truck that hit our house had come from? Or maybe they were all different Nairobis. It did not really matter: I was simply glad that now I could see and I would not have to endure razor blade incisions on my eyelids or have people call me Gacici. But I was even more amazed that my mother, who had never been to Nairobi without a helping companion, had guided me through it all. Surely my mother could do anything to which she set her mind.

Eyes healed, I was able to go back to the games of my childhood with greater freedom and enjoyment. One of the games my bad eyes would not have allowed me to play involved sliding down a hillside seated on a board along a slippery path smoothed with water the boys had drawn from the Manguo marshes. The slippery path ended just above a dirt road used by motor vehicles. The idea was to go down as fast as one could and then suddenly veer to the left or right just before the road. The whole thing needed good eyes to avoid possible collision with a passing motorcar. Now I was able to play the sport. It was dangerous but exhilarating, and at the end of the day I would be covered with mud. My mother promptly forbade it, reprimanding me for teaching my younger brother bad habits.

We also played a kind of pool; the ground was the table, and in place of four holes there was only one. Two competitors, each with six bottle tops in hand, would stand at an agreed-upon distance and throw the lot into the hole by turns, the idea being to get as many as possible into the hole with the first throw. As for the ones that missed the hole, each player, with a striker, a bottle top packed with mud to make it heavy, would try to hit them into the hole. The winner collected bottle tops from the defeated. The player with the highest score was the champion awaiting challengers with their own six bottle tops. There were boys who remained unconquered champions for days and in time attracted challengers from other villagers. I was never good at this because it involved good eye-hand coordination. This particular game, when in season, was addictive and often made some boys neglect their household chores in the pursuit of fame through the accumulation of bottle tops. Sometimes the most skilled played for money. My mother was very firm against our playing it.

My mother disliked any games that involved crowds of boys away from home. She wanted us to confine ourselves to those that could be played in our yard, like jumping rope and playing hopscotch, but my younger brother and I were no match for our half sisters and their friends. Jumping rope, they could do the most intricate tricks.

Like children elsewhere, I imagined airplanes. I would take a single dry blade of corn, an inch long and half an inch wide, and bore a hole in the middle through which I put a thin Y-shaped twig for steering. As I held the long end of the stick and ran against the wind the blade turned round and round, and the harder I ran the faster it spun. My brother made his own airplane the same way. We became pilots racing each other, making intricate aerial formations and maneuvers. This was fun. I did not have to squint in order to see.

We also made spinning tops, which we spun by hitting the

sides with a small strap made out of sisal strings. Here, the aim was to see who could keep his top spinning the longest, but sometimes it included racing the top over a particular distance to be the first to cross the finish line. More intricate maneuvers included trying to knock your opponent's top with yours while yours kept spinning.

We progressed to more challenging designs and engineering: making toy bicycles, cars, trucks, buses with all the parts—the body, wheels, steering—driven by manpower instead of internal combustion engines. Some kids added toy cyclists, drivers, and passengers. We would assemble on country tracks and open places to display our works but also to note the best designs to incorporate some of the ideas into our own future creations.

But we also learned to make useful toys. Mother having no younger daughters, we did for her what the young daughters of our age did for their mothers: fetching and carrying firewood on our back with a strap hanging from our forehead. Men did not carry loads that way; they did it on their heads or shoulders. So this earned us the title of "mother's girls." It was meant to be praise but I did not like the expression. So we sought a manlier alternative that would not involve our backs, shoulders, or heads. A carriage! Since we could not afford a wheelbarrow like the ones we saw at the landlord's and at the Indian shopping center, we decided to make one out of wood. We got a thick piece, chopped it, curved it all round with a machete, and then made a hole in the middle for the cog. We made the body entirely out of wood. But we never succeeded in making our wheelbarrow serviceable, especially on loose soil when the wheel would dig into the earth, or in rainy weather when it would get stuck in the mud. We had to have a proper iron wheel. A boy named Gacĩgua offered to get us a real one, a secondhand wheel rescued from old wheelbarrows, for thirty cents. But even one cent was hard to come by.

I would have to try my hand at picking tea. I begged my older sisters to let me accompany them to a tea plantation owned by a white man nicknamed Gacurio because he wore trousers with suspenders over his belly. Tea seeds from India were first introduced in Limuru in 1903, but to me, looking at the vast endless greenery in front of me, it looked as if the tea bushes had been part of this landscape from the beginning of time. An African overseer assigned the rows to be picked to different workers. Limuru was chilly and often subject to thin sheets of rain. Sisal sacks hanging from our heads served as raincoats. This task proved too difficult for me; I could hardly reach the top of the tea bushes, and I could not pluck them the way the experienced hands were able to do. They could pluck the leaves and expertly throw them over their shoulders into a huge basket on their backs. I did not have a basket of my own, and I became more of a nuisance, always in the way, and my sisters did not take me with them again. Despite my need for thirty cents, I did not insist.

It was easier with pyrethrum flowers, and when the season came I went with the older brothers and sisters to harvest at the landlord's, and this time my younger brother also came along. Still, it was hard: It took the whole day for us to fill just a small sisal basket.

I don't know how long it took, but eventually we managed to earn enough money to pay for the iron wheel. The owner raised the required fee. I was so anxious to get the wheel that I gave the money I had as down payment, but by the time I raised the rest the wheel was no longer available and it was he who now owed me money. He promised to get us another wheel. Disappointed, we resumed our engineering efforts and eventually came up with a better and smoother-functioning wheel. We then collected wood, nails, and wires from wherever we could and managed to make a semblance of a wheelbarrow. Equipped with our new vastly improved contraption, we would trek distances to collect firewood or fetch water in a tin container. Quite often the wheel would not move straight, especially on rough, uneven surfaces, and it needed the power of us two, one in front pulling with a rope and one behind pushing by the handles.

We took our home contraption everywhere, even to the pyrethrum fields, where it attracted the attention of other kids, particularly Njimi and Gĩtaũ, the young sons of the landlord, who often came to the fields, not to work, but for the company of age-mates, breaking the monotony of home confinement. They marveled at our contraption and they begged to push it. We were reluctant to let others touch it, so they brought us a real wheelbarrow to substitute for ours. What a difference between the real thing and our invention! But ours had the attraction of a homemade toy!

We used the demand for our toy to extract other privileges. The pyrethrum fields had not eaten up all the forest. It was still thick with bush. We would go there to climb trees, sometimes building bridges between them by connecting the branches of one tree with those of another, or using the branches to swing from tree to tree. What we most longed for was to hunt and capture a hare, or even an antelope. An antelope was once spotted in the pyrethrum fields and the entire workforce stopped what it was doing to chase the animal, shouting, Catch the antelope, but the animal was too fast for the screaming pursuers. We had often heard of boys who had managed to land one or the other, but it was clear from this experience that without a dog to help us, we would never manage to catch a hare, let alone an antelope. In exchange for the right to push our wheelbarrow, we persuaded Njimi and Gĩtaũ to bring their dogs to help us catch an animal and carry its carcass home on the wheelbarrow. We were lucky and spotted a hare and, led by the dogs, we immediately started chasing it. Soon the dogs and the hare left us behind, but the barking led us to a thick thorny bush. The dogs were barking at the bush, inside which a very frightened hare was ensconced, and no amount of stones thrown inside or shaking of the bush would persuade the hare to leave its lair. We never captured a hare, and after some time the novelty of the homemade wheelbarrow wore off for Njimi and Gĩtaũ, and the privilege of pushing it was worthless to us. My brother and I longed to have dogs that would be at our command anytime we wanted to hunt, or dogs that would follow us as we piloted our airplanes.

But the wheelbarrow had not yet lost its charm for those who saw it for the first time. An Indian boy became smitten by its toy power. The Indian community kept to itself, connected to Africans and whites only through its shops. In the front was the Indian merchant. Otherwise family life was in the backyard, each surrounded by high stone walls. Similarly high walls surrounded even the schoolyard. The only African people who had glimpses of the life of an Indian family were cleaners and sweepers, who said that Indians were of many nationalities, religions, and languages—Sikhs, Jains, Hindus, Gujaratis. They talked of conflicts between and within families, contradicting the image of seeming harmony. There was even less contact between Indian and African kids. Sometimes when a few of them ventured outside beyond the shops, African boys would throw stones at them for the joy of seeing them retreat to their barricaded backyards. From inside the barricades, they would also throw back stones. The most feared were the turbaned Sikhs because it was said they carried swords and when they ran back inside their yards we assumed it was to get their dangerous weapons. But children's curiosity about one another sometimes overcame the barriers of stone walls and adult warnings. That was how our wobbly homemade wheelbarrow attracted the eyes of the Indian boy who begged to be allowed to push it. He smoothed the way by giving us two tiny multicolored marbles. Later it took the occasional gift of a candy to bridge the human divide. And finally some kind of friendship was sealed by the gift of two puppies whose mother had given birth to too large a litter.

At long last we had dogs we could call our own. We brought them home in triumph, but my mother hated dog shit so much that she put them in a basket and took them back to the Indian shopping center and set them loose. We told our Indian friend that the puppies had escaped and he gave us another one. We tried to bring up the puppy secretly by building a dog pen in the bush around the dump site. We fed it in secrecy, but our mother must have been on to us. One day we woke up to find the puppy gone. We never saw our generous Indian friend again, and we could not go knock at his door to ask for him. Besides, what could we tell him? That the puppy had run away again?

I would soon be cured of any love for dogs. I was going to the pyrethrum fields one day, crossing the path to the landlord's house, when his dogs, the same dogs that had been our companions in hunting, came barking at me. I ran for dear life, but the dogs felled me and one of them dug its teeth into my leg just above the right ankle, a bite that left a scar and a lifelong fear of dogs.

I recalled and identified with the terror of the hare we had earlier tried to catch. I would leave hunting alone and stick to my homemade toys.

One evening, my mother asked me: Would you like to go to school? It was in 1947. I can't recall the day or the month. I remember being wordless at first. But the question and the scene were forever engraved in my mind.

Even before Kabae was demobilized, most of the sons younger than he, including my elder brother, Wallace Mwangi, had entered school, most of them dropping out after a year or two, because of the price of tuition. The girls, so bright, fared even worse, attending school for less than a year, a few of them teaching themselves at home and learning enough to be able to read the Bible. School was way beyond me, something for those older than I or those who came from a wealthy family. I never thought about it as a possibility for me.

So I had nursed the desire for schooling in silence. Though its seed had been planted by the status of my half brother Kabae in my father's house, its growth was influenced less by his example or that of my own brother Wallace Mwangi than by the children of Lord Reverend Kahahu: Njambi, the girl, and Njimi, a son, both about my age. When I worked in their father's fields harvesting pyrethrum flowers, I had often interacted with them, but I never imagined that I could ever be of their world. In lifestyle we inhabited opposite spheres.

The Kahahu estate of motor vehicles, churchgoing, economic power, and modernity was a contrast to ours, a reservation of hard work, poverty, and tradition, despite Kabae's glorious exploits and my father's wealth in cows and goats and his lip service to our ancestry. The difference between our clothes and those the Kahahu children wore was glaring: The girls had dresses; most of my sisters wore white cotton cloth wraps, sometimes dyed blue, over a skirt, the long side edges held together by safety pins and a belt of knitted wool. The young Kahahu boys' shirts and khaki shorts, held in place by suspenders, were a contrast to my single piece of rectangular cotton cloth, one side under my left armpit and with the two corners tied into a knot over the right shoulder. No shorts, no underwear. When my younger brother and I ran down the ridge, playing our games, the wind would transform our garments into wings trailing our naked bodies. I associated school with khaki wear, shorts, suspenders, and shoulder flaps. As my mother now dangled school in front of me, the uniform also came into view.

It was the offer of the impossible that deprived me of words. My mother had to ask the question again.

"Yes, yes," I said quickly in case she changed her mind.

"You know we are poor."

"Yes."

"And so you may not always get a midday meal?"

"Yes, Mother."

"Promise me that you'll not bring shame to me by one day refusing to go to school because of hunger or other hardships?"

"Yes, yes!"

"And that you will always try your best?"

I would have promised anything at that moment. But when I looked at her and said yes, I knew deep inside me that she and I had made a pact: I would always try my best whatever the hardship, whatever the barrier.

"You will start in Kamandũra school."

I don't know why my mother chose Kamandũra, where the children of the landlord went, rather than Manguo school, which my brother Wallace Mwangi had attended. It may have been because of differences in tuition, or because my uncle Gĩcini, much older than I, went to Kamandũra and he would look after me. I suspect that my mother had come to trust Lord Reverend Kahahu on account of his role in helping heal my eyes and that she was acting on his advice. I did not mind this choice because then I would be sure to have a school uniform like the children of the landlord.

My father had no say one way or another in this enterprise. It was my mother's dream and her entire doing. She raised the money for the tuition and the uniform by selling her produce in the market. And then one day she took me to the Indian shopping center. I had been there before, but I had not seen the shops as having anything to do with me directly except that some of the shops stocked rocks of unprocessed sugar—gur or jaggery or *cukari wa nguru* as we called it—which we bought for a few cents, our candy.

But now I saw the shops advertised as Shah Emporium or Draperies in a different light: They contained what would fulfill my desire. Eventually we made our way to a store that specialized in school wear. On the wall hung a picture of a thin Indian man wearing glasses. He seemed to be dressed in a cotton cloth serving as both his trousers and his shirt. How so, I thought, wondering whether I could have fashioned my garment so as to cover my body the same way. My mother bought me a shirt and a pair of shorts, the plainest, without suspenders or shoulder flaps, but lack of these adornments did not diminish my joy. I forgot to ask my mother who the frail-looking Indian was and why his picture hung on the wall. I was lost in contemplation of my new possessions. My only disappointment was that I would have to wait for school to start before I could wear them. And then at last!

The day I wear my khaki uniform and walk two miles to Kamandŭra is when I enter and float in the soft mist of a dreamland. I am in the mist as Njambi, the landlord's youngest daughter, who has guided me to school on the first day, shows me my starting class, sub B, taught by her older sister, Joana. The teachers are characters in a dream. Big-eyed Isaac Kuria is registering new pupils. He asks me my name. I say Ngũgĩ wa Wanjikũ, because at home I identified with my mother. I am puzzled when this is greeted with giggles in the class. Then he asks me: What's your father's name, and I say, Thiong'o. Ngũgĩ wa Thiong'o is the identity I shall carry throughout this school, but I am not conflicted by the two ways of identifying myself.

Later, I learn that sub B and A are a kind of preprimary

stage, slightly lower than grade one, or standard one, as it was called. I have entered sub B in the last third, so the others have been at it for the first two quarters. Njambi is already in grade one, two classes ahead, so she cannot help me navigate my way in this class. We sit on benches without desks or tables. The three classes are held at the same time in a church of corrugated iron walls and roof but in different spaces without any partitions. I can hear and see everything that is going on in the other spaces, but, as I soon learn, woe to anyone caught paying attention to what is going on outside one's space. But it is hard not to look since most of the teaching takes the form of call-and-response, the teacher writing and reading aloud some numbers or an alphabet on the blackboard, the kids repeating after him or her, in a singsong. Everyone, the teachers, the students, looks splendid in their strangeness.

I returned home in the evening, still in the dream, only to wake up to reality. I had to take off the school uniform and change into my usual garb. This became routine. Initially this was okay, but I soon found embarrassment increasingly creeping into my awareness of the world, especially when I encountered the other kids who had simply changed into regular shorts and shirts. But taking care of my school clothes was one of the promises I had made to my mother. She washed the one set of shirt and shorts every weekend so I could don them on Mondays. When I dirtied the clothes on weekdays, she would wash and dry them by the fire at night.

School remains an environment totally different from

the one of my ordinary living. I feel an outsider in our world, to which everyone else seems to belong. There are many things I don't understand. But one custom among the kids and teachers puzzles me. Before splitting into the different spaces, all the children assemble in the same place, bend their heads down, close their eyes, and the teacher says something like, Our Father who art in Heaven, and the entire assembly takes up the rest. I don't close my eyes. I want to see everything. But even after the Amen, some kids continue murmuring something to themselves, eyes still closed. For a long time this habit continues to puzzle me, and at one time I elbow one of the kids next to me to see if he would open his eyes, but he keeps them shut. Soon I figure out that the children are muttering a silent prayer. In my home we never prayed silently and individually. When my father used to live in the compound, he would wake up in the morning, stand in the yard facing Mount Kenya, pour a little libation, and say some words that ended with a loud call for peace and blessings for the entire household. Later I learn to shut my eyes but I don't have anything to mutter about. It was more fun with my eyes open, for there is a lot more to hold my attention.

I have bought a black slate and a white chalk for my writing material. We copy on our slates what the teacher has written on the blackboard. Later she comes around to grade on the slate, putting an X or a check against each word or number, totals them up, and then circles the cumulative number. At first I do not realize that after she has graded I still have to wait for her to enter the number in a register for the record. I rub off my work as soon as the teacher has graded it, but when I go home and my mother asks me what and how I had done and I say I rubbed off everything she says: Then don't, wait for the teacher to tell you what to do. The teacher also corrects me, otherwise I would continue getting zero, and when later she starts writing on my slate 10/10, and my mother asks me what I had done and I say, ten out of ten, she would ask probing questions ending with: Is that the best you could have done? This is a question she will keep on asking in response to my schoolwork, class exercises, and tests: Is that the best you could have done? Even when I tell her proudly that I scored ten out of ten, she asks the question in different ways, until I say yes, I had tried my best. Strange, she seems more interested in the process of getting there than the actual results.

I drift through the initial classes, not quite understanding why I have been moved from sub B to sub A to grade one, all within the same quarter, a skipping of classes that continues from term to term so that within a year I am in grade two, and still my mother continues to ask: Is that the best you could have done?

I don't know about the best that I could have done; all I know is that one day I am able to read on my own the Gĩkũyũ primer we used in class titled *Mũthomere wa Gĩkũyũ*. Some sentences are simple, like the one captioning a drawing of a man, an ax on the ground, his face grimacing with pain as he holds his left knee in both hands, drops of blood trickling down. The picture is more interesting than the words: *Kamau etemete. Etemete Kuguru. Etemete na ithanwa!* Kamau has cut himself. He has cut his leg. He has cut himself with an ax! I tackle long passages that do not have illustrations. There is a passage that I read over and over again, and suddenly, one day, I start hearing music in the words:

God has given the Agĩkũyũ a beautiful country
Abundant in water, food and luscious bush
The Agĩkũyũ should praise the Lord all the time
For he has ever been generous to them

Even when not reading it, I can hear the music. The choice and arrangements of the words, the cadence, I can't pick any one thing that makes it so beautiful and long-lived in my memory. I realize that even written words can carry the music I loved in stories, particularly the choric melody. And yet this is not a story; it is a descriptive statement. It does not carry an illustration. It is a picture in itself and yet more than a picture and a description. It is music. Written words can also sing.

And then one day I come across a copy of the Old Testament, it may have belonged to Kabae, and the moment I find that I am able to read it it becomes my book of magic with the capacity to tell me stories even when I'm alone, night or day. I don't have to wait for the sessions at Wangarĩ's in order to hear a story. I read the Old Testament everywhere at any time of day or night, after I have finished my chores. The biblical characters become my companions. Some stories are terrifying, like that of Cain killing his brother Abel. One night at Wangarĩ's their story becomes the subject of heated discussion. The story, as it emerges in this setting, is a little different from the one I have read about but it is no less terrifying. In this version Cain is condemned to wander the universe forever. He carries the mark of evil on his forehead and travels at night, a tall figure whose head scrapes the sky. Some of the storytellers claim that late one night they had encountered him and they ran home in terror.

Most vivid in a positive way is the story of David. There is David playing the harp to a King Saul of contradictory moods. Their alternations of love and hate are almost hard to bear. Years later I would completely identify with the lines of the spiritual: *Little David play on your harp.* But David the harpist, the poet, the singer is also a warrior who can handle slingshots against Goliath. He, the victor over giants, is like trickster Hare, in the stories told at Wangarĩ's, who could always outsmart stronger brutes. When later I learned how to make a sling attached to a Y-shaped twig, I would be thinking of David's, though I never met my Goliath in war. David, the warrior-poet, remains an ideal in my mind.

Some acts and scenes are simply magic within magic: Jonah swallowed by a whale and then vomited out unhurt on another shore; Shadrach, Meshach, and Abednego, an angel among them, walking about unscathed in a fiery furnace; Daniel interpreting correctly the writing on the wall—MENE, TEKEL, and PERES—which made me look for writings on walls so I could interpret them; and Daniel in a lion's den, emerging unhurt; or Joshua blowing a horn that brings down the walls of Jericho. Some of these images are powerful and remain imprinted in my mind. I now understand why Christians at Kamandŭra would always start prayers by invoking the God of Abraham and Isaac.

Nighttime frustrates me because I read by the light of an unreliable and coverless kerosene lantern. Paraffin means money and there are days when the lamp has no oil. Most times I rely on the firelight of an unreliable duration. Daylight is always welcome. It allows the book of magic to tell me stories without interruptions except when I have to do this or that chore. This ability to escape into a world of magic is worth my having gone to school. Thank you, Mother, thank you. The school has opened my eyes. When later in church I hear the words *I was blind and now I see,* from the hymn "Amazing Grace," I remember Kamandŭra School, and the day I learned to read.

But why does one recall some events and characters vividly and others not at all? How is the mind able to select what it buries deep in the memory and what it allows to float on the surface? Some students at Kamandŭra still stand out in my mind. There was Lizzie Nyambura, Kĩhĩka's daughter, in grade five, reputed to be brighter than even the teachers themselves, and who years later would be the first woman or man in the region to be admitted to Makerere University College to major in mathematics. Her brother Burton Kĩhĩka was reputed to be the fastest runner in the school and years later continued to indulge his love of speed by racing down the highways on a motorcycle with several falls and narrow escapes. There was Njambi Kahahu, my early guide, who later went to Alliance Girls and then on to the USA, married, and then died tragically while giving birth.

There was one Ndũng'ũ wa Livingstone with suspenders, one of which always fell off his shoulder to hang loosely on the side, and who had the only slate with lines indented, and whose handwriting was held up as exemplary. There was Mũmbi wa Mbero, who years later would be the first woman or man to ride a scooter in our town. And there was Mary, later married to Kĩbũthũ, Mũmbi's brother, who used to wrestle big boys to the ground. Throughout my stay in Kamandũra, I was terrified of her, I would avoid her, and I don't think I ever spoke to her, even once. There were Wamithi wa Umarĩ (Hamisi Omari, who years later would marry Wanja, one of my half sisters) and Juma, who came from Muslim families, and though they attended a Christian school, the fact never seemed to bother them or anybody else.

But children could also be very cruel, pitiless bullies, as in the case of Igogo. He was very tall, taller and older than the other kids. His name meant "Crow" or "Blackbird." Some children would gang together and when near him would crow like a bird. This used to annoy him, but when he ran toward them in anger they would simply scatter in different directions. Some days he would become very exhausted from having to chase his tormentors before deciding to run home, a lone figure with children in bushes and others following him at a distance singing his name in different pitches of mockery. He could not get help from the teachers: How could they forbid children to imitate a crow? In the end he stopped going to school, and, whatever his other reasons, this collective cruelty was a contributing factor.

Many of the teachers at Kamandūra are silhouettes in my memory, though I recall large-eyed Isaac Kuria, who registered me as the son of my father rather than my mother. There was also Paul Kahahu, who would later figure in the fortunes of my extended family; his sister, Joana, whom I credit with helping me to learn to read; and Rahabu Nyokabi Kĩambati, whom later offspring of families would also claim as their teacher. There is one teacher, Benson Kamau, nicknamed Gĩthuri, "Old Man," who used to sing out his lessons but with nonsensical lyrics like *Cows are property; money is property; goats are property* that became more and more absurdly monotonous by their repetition—but they stayed in the mind.

One event I always recall with heartache. I was in grade one when Teacher Joana selected me to join a performance group that would recite from memory the Beatitudes from the Gospel of Matthew and another passage from Mark at the end-of-year assembly for students and parents. I committed the whole passages to memory. They were poetic. They were music. I looked forward to it. I dreamed about it. But on the day of performance I left home a little late and arrived just as the group was saying: *And they brought young children to him, that he should touch them, and his disciples rebuked those that brought them. But when Jesus saw them he was much displeased, and said unto them, suffer the little children to come unto me and forbid them not, for such is the kingdom of God.*

The failure to perform left a hole in me, the need for a second chance to redeem myself to myself. For the duration of my stay in the school I always hoped that such a chance would present itself.

It never did. One day my elder brother Wallace Mwangi, with my mother apparently in agreement, told me that I had to leave Kamandũra for Manguo. It was very sudden, unexpected. It was the end of 1948, and I had been in Kamandũra for only two years, or, more precisely, one and a half, because I started there in the last quarter of 1947. I had many questions but I knew this would end an important phase of my life. The alternation between dream and reality that was my Kamandũra period was over, but I would forever carry in me the magic of learning to read and also the memory of loss. Perhaps the unknown Manguo would add to the magic of reading, and even soothe the ache of loss, but I doubted it could ever fill the hole.

Manguo was a short distance away: It stood on the ridge opposite our home, father's homestead; one went down the slope of our ridge, a narrow valley near the Manguo marshes, then up the next, Kĩeya's ridge, to the compound. The shorter distance and the news that my younger brother would be starting school at Manguo were enough to cheer me, and I started feeling good about the change.

Njinjũ was special to me and remained so even after I realized that my tears had had nothing to do with his coming into the world. But sibling rivalry for our mother's affection always produced tension between us. Sharing the same bed with my mother, we had often fought to be the one next to Mother's breasts. But moments of tension would alternate with those of extreme affection when we would share everything, a banana, a sweet potato, biting into them by turns, happily. But a few days later there would be accusations and counteraccusations about who had taken the bigger bites or who had taken an unfair turn; Mother would settle this by admonishing us to love each other as brothers, and then would follow a little talk on the importance of family. She did not have to convince us: We were at once brothers and best friends.

Once, soon after transferring to Manguo, I jumped over a low barbed wire fence around the school. One of the barbs caught the top of my left foot and tore deep into the flesh. Later it swelled and hurt so much that I could not walk. There were no medical clinics around and no doctor we could pay. My mother simply kept on washing the wound with salt water. My brother would literally cart me from place to place on the wheelbarrow. Somehow after weeks of my mother nursing my foot, I managed to begin walking again. An inch-long scar remains to this day. And a well of gratitude, for years later I learned of a child who had died of a similar wound, through tetanus poisoning.

But this memory and my love for Njinjũ became tinged with guilt brought about by my new clothes. I had grown used to khaki shorts in school, even as at home I continued to wear my traditional free-flowing garment knotted at the right shoulder, as did my brother, who only occasionally wore shorts underneath. By now my brother and I were inseparable. I often tried to teach him what I had learned in school, but he would resist, especially as he himself was going to start school and learn directly from proper teachers as I had done. He wanted respect as an equal; I wanted a younger brother to look up to me.

One weekend when there were sports on the grounds of the Limuru Bata Shoe Company, I was allowed to put on my school uniform. My brother, who had not yet started school and therefore had no uniform, simply put on shorts and knotted his garment. Sports festivals were always much fun. I loved races best of all, especially the long distances, a mile or more, fascinated as I was by the pacing and changing of tactics. Many contestants would start together. Then a few would pull ahead, and toward the end two or three would finally separate themselves from all the others and struggle to beat each other to the tape. In the long distances, leaders would keep on changing, some literally coming from way behind, even overtaking others and passing them by a lap. My brother and I found fun walking around the sports field mingling with the crowds. And that was how, ahead of me, I saw some students I did not even know well, coming toward me. Suddenly I was aware, as if for the first time, that my brother was in his traditional garb.

The embarrassment that had been seeping into my consciousness of the world around me since I first wore new clothes to school came back intensely. Panic seized me. I did the only thing that I thought would save the situation. I asked my brother whether we could take two different paths around the field and see who would get to the other side first. My brother and I were used to such friendly rivalries and he readily took up the challenge. Well, I passed the other uniformed kids. They did not once look at me, one way or another. After all, I was new to the school. By the time my brother and I met, I was already remorseful, while he was bubbling with joy at having beaten me to the spot. My behavior ruined the rest of the day for me. I might have found my predicament easier to bear if I had voiced it to my brother. But I didn't and it remained and it would not go away. The problem, I came to realize, was not in my brother or the other boys but in me. It was inside me. I had lost touch with who I was and where I came from. Belief in yourself is more important than endless worries of what others think of you. Value yourself and others will value you. Validation is best that comes from within. In later tribulations, this thought always helped me to endure and overcome challenges by relying on my own will and resolve even when others were skeptical of me. More important, it made me realize that education and lifestyle could influence judgment in a negative way and separate people.

In compensation, I felt and became even more protective of and closer to my younger brother. I looked forward more intensely to his joining me at Manguo. I would make sure that nothing came between us.

We were hardly two terms in the new school when temptation, in the form of a train, challenged my commitment to school.

One evening my mother told my younger brother and me that she would be leaving for a few days. She was going to Elburgon, Warubaga as we called it, in the Rift Valley, to visit with my grandmother Gathoni; her uncle, Daudi Gatune; and her sister, Auntie Wanjirũ. The other women would look after us and she wanted assurance of good behavior while she was away. The decision was sudden, and my mother seemed more anxious than happy about the prospective journey.

I had heard of my maternal grandmother living far away with Auntie Wanjirũ. But they were just names to me because I had never met them in the flesh or if I had I could not recall. But the moment my mother added that she was going to go there by train, the scene changed dramatically. We both wanted to accompany her. You cannot leave us behind, we cried. But we were in the middle of a school year and my younger brother had just started school. Yes, but Mother, you cannot leave us behind. I don't need your tears, she finally said. It is your choice, whether or not you want to leave school and come with me. You have three days to think about it!

The railway line, which was started in 1896 in Kilindini, Mombasa, and reached Kisumu in December 1901 through the Kenyan heartland, had brought in its wake not only European settlers but also Indian workers, some of whom opened shops at the major construction camps that later bloomed into railroad towns. It also created the native African worker out of the peasant who, having lost his land, had only the power of his limbs that he hired out to the white settler, when his labor was not taken by force, and to the Indian *dukawallah*, or shopkeeper, for a pittance. The land over which he had been the sovereign became divided into White Highlands for Europeans only, the Crown lands owned by the colonial state on behalf of the British king, and the African Reservations for the natives. The Indians, not allowed to own land, became merchant dwellers in the big and smaller railroad towns between Mombasa and Kisumu. The railway line was the link between these towns long before the road built by the Bonos provided competition. This was the same railway line that had once terrified my father and his older brother but was now so normal a part of the landscape that my mother was talking about taking the train, with us clamoring to join her.

I cannot overstate the lure of the Sunday passenger train from Mombasa to Kisumu or Kampala. It always made a stop at Limuru, where the railway station was opened on November 10, 1899. The train usually arrived at midday. Europeans and Indians came there to meet relatives and say good-bye to others. Some Africans also came to do the same. But most Africans wandered there to see the train come and go, the young left to loiter and mingle on the platform. The train whistle could be heard from our homestead, and even the smoke could be seen snaking its way in the sky when one stood on top of the dump site. Every Sunday my older sisters and brothers would wake up and get ready, not for church or native festivities, but for the train. Some sat in little groups in the huge compound, fussing over each other's hair while others washed their feet in basins and smoothed their nails and heels with a scrubbing stone. The compound was a flurry of noisy activities, as friends from neighboring villages sometimes came to see if everyone was ready to go to the platform together.

There is one Sunday forever imprinted in my mind. As usual my brothers and sisters had performed their ablutions and preparations early. But they had not timed themselves properly. Suddenly they heard the train hooting as it approached the station. We will be late for the train! came the cacophonous cry. Within seconds they had all taken to their heels, running down the slope as if in an athletic competition. Sisters Gathoni, Kageci, Nyagaki, and their friends Wamaitha and Nyagiko; half brothers Kangi, Mbici, and Mwangi wa Gacoki, the tallest of all my siblings, and others were running as if for their lives. My younger brother and the siblings about our age—Wanja, Wanjirũ wa Njeri, Gakuha, Gacungwa—stood on top of the dump site and enjoyed this race to the platform of the Limuru railway station.

When minutes later we heard the train leave the station, we started singing what we thought the train was saying: TO U-GA-NDA, TO U-GA-NDA, with the train seeming to acknowledge our song and dance with a prolonged hooting and smoke in the sky.

I had never been to the platform to witness the romance of the train, but of course we had heard many alluring stories about it. The passenger train was divided into sections: first class for Europeans only, second class for Indians only, and third class for Africans. I longed to be there, to see it all for myself. And here, at long last, was a chance not simply to stand on a platform and stare at a passing train, but to become a passenger myself. Why should I let school and my pact with Mother stand in the way?

True to her word, on the third day she posed the question and waited for our decision. My younger brother was prompt in his response. He would take the train; he would resume schooling afterward. It was now my turn. Would I let my younger brother be first to experience the magic of the train? But how could I leave school and live with the fact? I wished my mother would decide for me. There was no pressure from her either way. The choice was mine. Tears flowed down my cheeks. I could not bring myself to break the pact regarding school that I had made with Mother. I could not abandon my dreams. The train would have to pass me by!

In this phase of my life I inhabited a social space defined by Kahahu's house, Baba Mūkūrū's house, and my father's house. The three homesteads neighbored each other, though Baba Mūkūrū's was just a few yards outside the boundary of Kahahu's land. Though they could never erect insurmountable walls between them, the three centers represented three different models of modernity and tradition.

Lord Reverend Kahahu's modernity was visible in everything. He had had an elementary education, had trained as a reverend, and all his children attended school, two of them, Joana and Paul, becoming teachers. He always wore the white collar of his profession as a reverend; the entire family was always dressed in suits and dresses. He was the first to grow pyrethrum and an orchard of plums, the first to own oxen-pulled carriages and donkey-pulled carts, the first to introduce mule-pulled plows with the plowman at the handles, and the first to have a car and later a truck. His younger brother, Edward Matumbĩ, established the first wholly African-owned sawmill in the region. Lord Reverend Stanley Kahahu exuded modernity in his person and family.

Their homestead, however, remained a mystery to me.

I had never been beyond the outer gates. A thicket of pine trees surrounded the homestead, and I could only get glimpses of the house through gaps in the trees. But this changed when one day his wife, Lillian, invited the children of the families that worked on their land to a Christmas party.

Christians or not, we all celebrated Christmas. On Christmas Eve, children and young men and women moved from house to house, in the dark, with handheld glass-covered paraffin lanterns, singing carols. On the actual day, one did not wait for a special invitation to a neighbor's house for tea and homemade parathas. All homes, except those, like the Kahahus', that saw themselves as modern, were open to passing guests. Most of the homes made similar dishes: a vegetarian affair of curry broth with potatoes and beans or peas. It was not a matter of choice. Whenever families could afford to, they would add chicken, beef, or lamb into the curry. Most homes could not afford baked bread from the Indian shops. But all families were experts at making parathas. A few pounds of wheat flour could produce many of these flat breads. We stuffed ourselves with them, and I have always associated Christmas with parathas and curry. It was a festive season for all equally; there were no special parties for children. So to be invited to a children's Christmas party, moreover in the mysterious landlord's house, was something new in our lives. We tried to look our best. This was years before I had even dreamt of attending school and wearing shorts and shirts. My younger brother and I were still in our cloth apparel but Mother made sure we were clean.

We kept on exchanging glances, and we bonded regarding the scene before us. Everything was a revelation. There was this huge compound covered with grass that had been cut and trimmed low with nice well-defined paths that connected the various buildings, a contrast to our compound of sand and dust. The main house was a four-cornered building with walls of thick wood and a corrugated iron roof with drainage pipes leading to two tanks that collected rainwater at the corners. Separate from the main building was the kitchen, similarly built but smaller, with water draining into a smaller tank. I was a little disappointed that the party took place in the kitchen, spacious as it was, and not in the big house, but still the pile of jam sandwiches in huge containers made up for any shortcomings in location.

I thought that after the long welcoming preliminaries and the discourse on the meaning of Christmas we would immediately be served the tea and the gleaming white bread sandwiches. Instead we were told to shut our eyes for prayer. My brother and I had never said prayers, let alone one for food. Food was there to eat not to pray over. And why close our eyes? Lillian started what to me sounded like an endless monologue to God. In the middle of it I opened my eyes to peep at the pile of sandwiches. I met my brother's eyes doing the same. I quickly closed mine but after a while opened them again only to catch my brother doing the same. We knew exactly what the other was thinking about the endless prayer that stood between us and the food. We could not help it. We giggled loudly. Lillian was not amused.

Her eyes were cold, her tone chilly, as now she gave my brother and me a stern lecture on Christian etiquette. Her children had been trained in Christian ways, and they would never have done what we had done in the eyes of God, and if they had, she would not have allowed them to eat the bread or any food for days. But she would forgive us because, being heathens, we did not know any better. All the children's eyes, including Njambi's and Njimi's, were on us. The desire for the bread disappeared. Humiliated, I stood up and walked away. My brother followed me, but not before he had grabbed a couple of sandwiches.

I could not get relief by being angry with Lillian because deep inside I was ashamed of our behavior. Unchristian or not, what my brother and I had done was unbecoming. Besides, I still carried the memory of Lord Kahahu's generous intervention in the healing of my eye infection. My mother held a similar view. While admonishing us for our bad behavior, she was clear that it had nothing to do with not being Christian. She also seemed to make a distinction between Lillian and her husband, and she encouraged me to forget the offending phrase "not brought up in Christian ways." But the words would not go away. They were imprinted on my mind, and I was to hear them again after a clash between Kahahu and Baba Mũkũrũ.

Baba Mũkũrũ's house was antithetical to Kahahu's. He was as confident in the ways of his ancestors as Kahahu was in the ways of his Christian ancestors. For him, tradition was sacrosanct. He and his children observed all the rites of passage, not only initiations from one phase of life to another but also forms of social education. It was in his house that I once witnessed the ceremony of being born again.

Nyakanini, "Little One" as she was fondly known, was the last born of the girls of Baba Mũkũrũ with his second wife, Mbũthũ. She was much younger than I. At the age of six or so she was made to lie between her mother's legs in a fetal position. Amid songs from the semicircle of a chorus of women, Mbũthũ reenacted pregnancy and labor. The chorus members were also participatory witnesses. Some of them played midwives and brought Nyakanini into the world a second time. Gĩtiro was a poetic operatic form of improvisations, call-and-response, challenge and counter-challenge, narration of conflict and reconciliation. Baba Mũkũrũ poured a libation for the ancestral spirits that they might be with the living and the newly reborn. Nyakanini's mother, Mbũthũ, performed the symbolic feeding of the newborn. Again, through song and dance, we saw the child grow from babyhood to puberty. Still in performance mode, Nyakanini literally followed her mother to the fields, where they worked together picking greens and digging for potatoes. The chorus did not go with them, but when mother and daughter returned with their token harvest, they were welcomed with ululations. Though the actual cooking had been done, they symbolically reenacted the preparation with what they had brought from the fields. Nyakanini did everything that her mother did, but she was the one who initiated the sharing out of what had already been cooked, giving a little to her mother and the chorus, thereby suggesting that she had successfully moved from babyhood to the next stage of youth. If it had been a boy, he would have followed his father to the grazing fields and brought back some milk. At the end of the ritual, Nyakanini was a child approaching adulthood, at which stage she would undergo the initiation rites of circumcision. Finally a feast celebrated the young girl she had become, after being born again.

For Baba Mũkũrũ this was education enough, and he would not allow any of his kids to attend the mission school, let alone attend church services, although, ironically, one of his daughters with his first wife had married a Mũgĩkũyũ Muslim convert, and he had lost a son in the Second World War, the most modern of all wars. Another of his daughters, nicknamed Macani, "Tea Leaves," who had not been to school, adopted the latest in Western-style dresses; she was one of the few who could openly defy him without bad repercussions. But by that time her mother and Baba Mũkũrũ had separated.

He never wanted to have anything to do with the Kahahus who, for him, represented every negation, every betrayal of tradition. Even when some of his daughters, whose beauty was the talk of the young men, worked in Lord Reverend Kahahu's pyrethrum plantation, they did so secretly. He would rather they worked in the European-owned tea plantations than in the fields of a renegade.

Unfortunately for him a Romeo and Juliet affair was developing between one of his daughters, Wambũi, and Kahahu's eldest son, Paul. Like his father before him, Paul had graduated from Mambere, a Church of Scotland Mission primary school at Thogoto, Kikuyu, and worked as a teacher in Kamandŭra. He and Wambŭi had a secret liaison that was revealed by her pregnancy. Baba Mŭkŭrŭ followed custom and sent a delegation of elders to Kahahu's house to look into the matter. The Kahahus would not receive them: Our son has been brought up a Christian and would never do such a thing, Lillian was quoted as having said. Why, Lillian asked with cutting sarcasm, are you people unable to bring up your children the way we have done ours? Baba Mŭkŭrŭ was wounded, furious with the Kahahu family for backing their son in his denial of responsibility, and he vowed to pursue the matter even if it meant protesting outside the doors of the very church where Reverend Kahahu preached on Sundays and where the son taught on weekdays. But before Baba Mŭkŭrŭ could carry out his threats, the Kahahu family shipped Paul to a school in South Africa. The matter was not resolved, except that the girl to whom Wambŭi gave birth looked exactly like Paul Kahahu. This gorgeous little girl who united the two families was rejected by the heads of both. Paul's flight to South Africa, however, had the unintended effect of dramatizing overseas education in our region as both desirable and accessible. It also brought South Africa home to us and enhanced Kahahu's modernity.

Because my father stood aloof from the rituals of both tradition and Christianity, considering himself modern, he was haughty vis-à-vis Baba Mŭkŭrŭ and Lord Reverend Stanley alike. His attitude toward his brother may have been conditioned by his having rubbed shoulders with a white person in the big city, having worked as his servant. As to Kahahu, my father always thought himself the rightful owner of the land Kahahu occupied, and so in the reverend's preaching my father saw hypocrisy. Even the news of Paul Kahahu going to South Africa would not have fazed my father who, despite the fact that he did not actively embrace education, could still boast of a son, an ex-military man, who had been overseas and had come back with learning.

From Lord Reverend Kahahu I myself learned to revere modernity; from Baba Mũkũrũ, the values of tradition; and from my father, a healthy skepticism of both. But the performance aspects of both Christianity and tradition always appealed to me.

My father was known all over the region for having quality *mũratina*, a homemade wine made out of a mixture of the purest of sugarcane that he himself grew, the richest of honey, and the finest of natural yeast, stored in gourds that were finely cut and shaped. But he had developed remarkable discipline in how he used his time. He would never drink during the workday. Those invited for wine at his home on a weekend had to show respect for his wives and children. If they misbehaved, he would send them away. A revered patriarch, he nevertheless acknowledged that his wives headed their respective households.

In my mind, my father's patriarchy established itself in two distinct phases. I had a vague early childhood recollection of his kraal, a space surrounded by a fence of wood and an outer hedge of thorny bush, part of the homestead: images of his coming home in the evenings leading his enormous herd of cows into the vast kraal, sometimes aided by the older sons, or one of his wives, and then, after securing the herd inside, he would go to his *thingira*, equidistant to those of his four wives. He was careful not to show any preference for any one of his wives' huts. When the women brought him food, he would invite us children to share. We enjoyed a daily feast. He was not a great storyteller but he was keen on teaching us good eating habits, like not biting off more than we could chew, and not swallowing what was only hastily chewed. Take your time, the food is not going anywhere. Sometimes his fellow elders came to visit him, to deliberate issues of the moment. My father had one of the best smiles ever, but his laughter could also be ironic, sinister sounding at times, when he was reacting to matters of which he disapproved.

Although it was never clear to me how the transition occurred, the second phase followed my father's expulsion from the fields around the homestead, because now his hut was rarely occupied and we did not share meals with him anymore. The women still took food to him daily, but to the edges of my maternal grandfather's forest of blue gum and eucalyptus trees, not far from the Limuru African market shops. A new *thingira* was built next to his property, quite a distance from the old homestead. He came home mostly on Saturdays or Sundays when he had *mũratina* to share with his friends. If he stayed for the night, he would sleep in one of the women's huts.

I had always wanted to help in the herding like some of the older boys but he never asked me. One time, long before I started school, I had accompanied one of the boys, my half brother Njinjũ wa Njeri, to my father's new abode. Indians burned their dead among the eucalyptus and blue gums. My mother said that if you stood on the dump site at home, you could see Indian ghosts walking about, holding a light.

Have you seen the spirits with your own eyes? Yes, she would say, and described how on some nights she had seen the tiny light move to and fro in pitch darkness. Pressed for more details, if she had actually seen the body of the spirits for instance, she would close the subject, slightly irritated that we were questioning the veracity of an eyewitness account. She spoke with total conviction as if she were describing an encounter in the marketplace. I may not have believed her, but I was still a little scared of the place. The grounds were vast; the trees tall, the undergrowth thick in some places, and I assumed that the strange scent emanating from the trees and the undergrowth was really that of the burnt flesh of the Indian dead. The cattle and goats roamed everywhere but mostly at the outer edges of the forest, where there were long treeless patches. After a market day, my half brother would let the herds roam about in the African marketplace and sometimes let them eat the tall grass in the shops' backyards. The owners did not mind this because it saved them from having to cut it short. Through the forest, near my father's new kraal, was a path that led to the railway station and the Limuru marketplace. My half brother would stop some of the girls passing by and chat them up, asking them to "give it to my brother," pointing at me, vowing that I knew how to do it very well. The ladies would smile and walk away or call him names. I did not understand what he meant by those words or the girls' response. Whatever the case, it felt good just to hang around or go exploring inside the forest, not being particularly worried about where the goats and cows were, except in the evening when we collected them and led them back into the kraal and closed the gates. When I grew up, I thought, I would ask my father to let me be his regular assistant herd boy so that I would learn how to milk the cows the way my half brother did, and talk to the girls the way he did.

But I never got a chance, not only because I had started school but because a disaster struck. His goats and cows caught a strange illness. Their tummies puffed up, followed by diarrhea and death. Traditional medical expertise was no match for the disease. There were no veterinary services for African farmers at the time. His animals died one by one. Rumors swirled that his goats and cows had once strayed to the backyard of some tea shop in the African marketplace, and ate some of the clothes drying on a line and drank the clean water in containers. The irate owner, in vengeance, had later poisoned the grass and the water.

Whatever the explanation, the disaster that befell my father was long cited in arguments between proponents of holding money in banks and those who believed that livestock was the only real measure of wealth. One fact they would not dispute: The man who had everything had now lost all.

His loss of wealth devastated my father. The proud, aloof patriarch who had always left each wife to tend her house as she saw fit now tried to micromanage the entire homestead, even questioning the comings and goings of his daughters, saying aloud that he did not want any of them to go the way of Baba Mũkũrũ's daughter. His interference became worse after he abandoned his *thingira* near the empty kraal and moved into Njeri's, the youngest wife's, place, while insisting that the other wives deliver his food to him there. This upset the delicate balance of power that the women had worked out among themselves. When he tried to assuage the resulting tension among them, he only made it worse.

Although we all feared our father, I had never once seen him beat a child. If anything, he had been very strict about mothers beating children; he discouraged it, a very unusual attitude in those days. Also unusual was that he had seldom beaten his wives, yet he commanded their respect and his word was law. Now he engaged in domestic violence, particularly against my mother. The only woman he did not touch was Njeri. She was big-limbed, strong-bodied, and the story goes that once, when drunk, he tried to discipline her, but, with him inside the hut, she locked the door from inside to shut out eyewitnesses and beat him, while shouting, loudly enough for all the world to hear, that he was killing her. This was among many stories now bandied about to show how low he had sunk.

The proud patriarch who would never have gone to someone else's house to drink liquor unless invited, the man who would never have drunk on a weekday, now started drinking all the time, and, no longer brewing his own, going to other people's houses for *mũratina*. My father hated those husbands who waylaid their wives on their way from the market for a share of the money they had earned from their sales. But now he started doing just that. It was painful to see him waiting for the end of the week to demand the wages that his daughters, my sisters, had earned for working in the pyrethrum fields of Lord Stanley Kahahu or in the tea plantations in the White Highlands. They would dodge him, some even escaping into marriage.

He tried his hand at farming, but because he had no land of his own he still depended on the cultivation rights from his father-in-law, my maternal grandfather. Before he lost everything, he used to grow crops like sweet potatoes, arrowroot, sugarcane, and yams, on a parcel of land near the Indian shops, but more as a hobby than for subsistence. He was very proud of the quality of what he produced. His was a model garden. But now cultivation for subsistence was all. As he struggled to eke out a living from the soil, his sense of his manliness and public standing was compromised.

Good as he was with his hands turning the soil, he was

competing with his women, my mother particularly. His parcel of land was next to hers, and it was as if the playfulness of his wooing her had now become a serious competition between them for power. But when it came to coaxing the land to yield, not my father, not the other women, nobody was a match for my mother. She put mulch around the crops: Even with goats my mother now had an edge over my father. He had none; she had two he-goats that she fattened inside a pen in her hut. She had three others that she sometimes fed in the hut but that otherwise used to follow her wherever she went in daytime without straying.

The year she came back from the short visit to Elburgon with my younger brother saw her work magic on the land. While other people's crops seemed to wilt under the sun, hers bloomed. People sometimes stopped by the road to admire the peas, beans, and corn in her various parcels of land. By the end of the season, my mother had harvested just about the best crop of peas and beans in the region. Corn as well. Other women offered to help her harvest and shell, filling ten sacks with peas, four with beans, and her barn with corn, a feat that brought gawkers from nearby.

My father decided that the harvest was his to dispose of, even to sell. My mother, used to the independence of her household, firmly refused. One day he came home, picked a quarrel with her, and started beating her up, even using one of the walking sticks that my half sister Wabia used for support, till it broke into pieces. My brother and I were crying for him to stop. Mother was screaming in pain. Despite their fear, the other women tried to restrain him, beseeching him to stop, screaming in solidarity, for all the world to hear, that their husband had gone crazy. As he turned toward them in fury, my mother managed to slip away with only the clothes she wore, and fled to her father's house, my grandfather's, leaving behind her goats and harvest.

For many days after, the family talked about the beating, some even claiming that her goats had screamed in protest. Nobody seemed able to fully explain the fury that my father had shown. But there were whispers here and there that the cause of it was the youngest wife, Njeri, the only one who worked on the European-owned tea plantations. She was having an affair with one of the overseers. The women said that somehow my father had gotten it into his head that my mother was at fault. They surmised that because Njeri had once fought him, he took his anger and frustrations out on the easier target.

With the departure of our mother, the other wives, Gacoki and Wangarĩ in particular, took care of my brother and me. We waited for her to come back or for my father to go to his in-laws to plead with them for her return. That was the procedure: talks that would almost certainly end in warnings, fines, and reconciliation. Everybody knew that it was simply a matter of time. But my younger brother and I missed her terribly, and this sharing of a common loss and need made us even closer.

My younger brother used to talk about his journey by train. He enumerated with special emphasis the stations he had passed through, Naivasha, Gilgil, Nakuru, Molo, at least the ones he could remember. He even claimed that Kisumu and Kampala were very near Elburgon, and he would have gone there but for his busy life at Elburgon playing with Grandmother and Auntie Wanjirũ and her daughter, our cousin Beatrice. I learned from him that Auntie Wanjirũ, a trader, was a single parent. He talked about Grandmother's tenderness though without offering many details. His was a narrative I was not very keen to hear, and I would counter his triumphs by talking about my glorious days at school, a subject that he too was now not very keen to hear. Our unspoken contention became an undeclared duel; he exaggerated his exploits in Elburgon and I, my educational adventures in school. But he always got the better of me by reminding me that Mother had promised to sell some of her harvest for his tuition to resume schooling at the beginning of a new term. He would have schooling as well as the train experience. Even though I was envious of his journey, I was also happy that he would eventually join me in school. But as days came and went, we increasingly became anxious about Mother's return, our increasing anxiety tempered only by the daily routine of social life at our father's homestead.

One day my brother and I were playing with our siblings in an open space between Kahahu's land and Baba Mũkũrũ's with a ball made of cloth and tied tight with a string. Even the girls had joined in. My father suddenly turned up. He stood at a distance and beckoned my brother and me to accompany him. My father had never called me to him before, let alone come all the way to a field outside our homestead to do so. We ran to him, sure that he was going to tell us news of our mother's return.

I want you to stop playing with my children. Go, follow your mother, he said, pointing in the general direction of my grandfather's place.

We did not have a chance to say farewell to the other children and tell them that we had been banished from their company and from the place that up to then had defined our lives. But before leaving home, I was able to dash into my mother's hut to retrieve my school material, among which was my beloved torn copy of stories from the Old Testament.

The expulsion was, if not from paradise, from the only place I had known. I was baffled more than pained. My mother had always been the head of the immediate household, so home would always be wherever she was, and in that sense I was headed home to Mother. But it is not a good thing to have your own father deny you as one of his children. The move deepened my sense of myself as an outsider, a feeling I had harbored since I learned that the land on which our homestead stood was not really ours. I had been an outsider at Kamandūra, where it seemed that others belonged more than I did, and at Manguo upon moving there. Now I was an outsider in my father's house. But there are aspects of the old homestead that will always be a part of me: the story-telling sessions, daily interaction with the other children where alliances changed from time to time; fights and tears even. Some of the scenes flitted across my mind: the games we played, the songs we sang, and the dances in the yard wel-coming rain for it meant blessings and made the children grow. At the sighting of raindrops we dashed into the yard, formed a circle:

Rain may you fall
I offer you a sacrifice
A young bull with bells
That sound ding dong

Once a host of children, including my half sisters and
half brothers—Wanja, Gacoki's daughter; Gacungwa, Wangarĩ's daughter; and Gakuha and Wanjirũ, Njeri's son and
daughter—and I were playing the game of Catch Me If You
Can. I was running around each of the four huts, all of them
chasing after me, when suddenly I tripped over something
and fell. The sand scraped the skin off my left shoulder. The
scar remained; it will always be there, a memory. Now banished from my larger family by my father, I was lucky to have
my younger brother and the book of stories for companions
and the solace of reunion with my mother in her father's
place, the place of her birth.

I had met my maternal grandfather but only briefly.
Given the absence of her mother, who lived in Elburgon,
while her father lived in Limuru with Mũkami, his youngest
wife, my mother may not have felt the need to make frequent
visits. As for the children, our identity was always with the
family of our father and not the in-laws, even when one was
named after a relative on the mother's side. I was named
Ngũgĩ after my maternal grandfather. But my mother used
to call me Njogu, "Elephant," or the diminutive Mũkũgĩ, or
"Little Papa." Other women, particularly her co-wives,
always referred to her as "Ngũgĩ's daughter."

My grandfather was an imposing figure, dressed in a white undergarment, one side under his left arm, the ends pinned together over his right shoulder, a kind of one-sleeved tunic, and an equally long outer garment, a blanket of sorts, under the right arm and tied over his left shoulder. As Limuru was often cold and drizzly, particularly in July, he would sometimes wear a long coat over both. He was a big landowner in his own right, and, as the head and trustee of his entire Kamami subclan, he had flexibility over the rights of use of the clan's extensive patrimony. Unlike my father, whose ancestors had no roots in Limuru, my grandfather, his extended family, and his entire subclan did, owning and controlling acres of cultivated and virgin lands. After the death of one of his cousins, he had inherited two widows, so he was also the titular head of the Ndũng'ũ family. Ndũng'ũ's children, including Kĩmũchũ, the eldest, accepted and looked up to him as the head of the extended family. With Njango, the younger of the two widows, he had sired a son, Uncle Gĩcini. The whole web of family interconnections was a bit complicated, and I am not sure that I was able to understand all the nuances. The family lived in three different compounds in the same area.

Having separated from his first wife, Grandmother Gathoni, Grandpa Ngũgĩ may have wondered if they had passed the germ of separation onto their daughter, and he was probably at a loss as to what to do after my mother left my father. Custom demanded he wait for the husband to sue for the return of his wife, which would open the door for discussions. My mother lodged in Njango's hut, assumed to be a temporary arrangement by everyone. The arrival of my brother and me complicated matters.

My father may have thought that our presence would exert pressure on her to come back and sue for peace on his terms, but our appearance may have actually made it easier for her to stick to her decision not to return to his domestic violence. Without us there, she would have found it difficult to stay away. Now she wanted her father to allow her to put up a hut of her own on his land. He was cautious. Being wise in the ways of customary law and practices, he wanted to wait for my father to send a delegation for formal talks. After all, she had been married legally, my father had paid the required dowry, and divorce would mean my grandfather would have to give back the dowry, goats. Besides, the community had no procedure for the divorce of a couple with grown-up children like my older brothers and sisters. Divorce was not an option, only separation. So my mother lived in limbo, estranged from her husband's place and not quite accepted in her father's. She who had always enjoyed her independence now felt like a trapped animal, forced to live in a crowded hut, sharing a common cooking space with no utensil she could call her own, and without her own food, because her harvest had been taken from her.

I try to figure ways of helping her but I am actually more worried about tuition. I come up with a scheme to trade in school materials: pencils and slates and exercise books. My younger brother thinks I am a genius. I then approach Uncle Gĩcini. Gĩcini is only a couple years older than I, and I don't actually call him uncle. My other uncles, Gĩkonyo and Mũthoga, are older, with families, and I have always assumed that "uncle" is a term children use to honor those older than they are. But Gĩcini and I had even attended the same school, Kamandũra, though he had been a few classes ahead, so I think of him more as an equal than an uncle. He is excited about the idea, which now becomes a joint dream: buying pencils and erasers from the Indian shops and then selling them to needy schoolkids for a higher price. We start calculating the money we would make by continually re-investing the profit in more goods. Soon we are rich, in our minds, and this spurs us to realize our plans. At my grand-father's forest we cut down trees to create four corner posts and thin sticks for crossbeams. At first it is a secret, known only to Gĩcini and my younger brother, Njinjũ. But our enthusiasm knows no bounds, and we hint at the riches to Gĩcini's brother. He does not laugh at the idea. Instead he tells us a story of a poor man whose chicken laid two eggs. He was hungry but he restrained himself, collected them in a bowl, sat in a chair, and closed his eyes to work out what to do with them. He would take them to market, he thought to himself, still leaning back in his chair, the bowl on the floor. With the money, he would buy some more eggs and sell them at a profit, buy some more till he had a pile. He would reinvest all the money into buying and selling other things, again at a profit. Soon, in his mind, he ended up owning a house and getting married. He and his wife lived happily until one day they had a small dispute and his wife answered back. He got so angry at her perceived ingratitude that he kicked her. He hit the bowl and the eggs were yolk and broken shells. Stop daydreaming. How many pencils are you likely to sell? How many kids go to school around here? Why would anybody refuse to buy cheaply at the Indian shops only to walk all the way to a forsaken place to buy the same things more dearly? He has deflated our dreams of easy riches. The structure of four posts and a few crossbeams stands there for many months, a forlorn monument to a dream.

Uncle Gĩcini feels guilty about our collapsed scheme. He tries to mollify me by offering to teach me how to catch moles. Moles are a scourge to farmers. They eat plant roots, and after a while you can see the mounds they make and the desolation. The mole is an invisible enemy because it travels underground. How can one catch such a creature? Easy, he tells me. A trap: a piece of wood, hollow inside, three strings, two are nooses at both ends, and the middle, carrying the bait, is firm. Dig a trench and place the trap in the mole's path, cover it with soil, and then tie the strings to a bent elastic stick in the earth aboveground. As the mole goes through the noose to eat the bait in the middle, the stick straightens up, and the noose tightens around the mole. I don't believe him but we try anyway. We make two traps, one for me. His fails. Mine catches a mole at the first attempt. News of my skill spreads. I become a professional mole catcher, charging a fee, and earning gratitude from the farmers. I might even become a hero, like the rat catcher of the village legend.

There was a period, during our lives in my father's homestead, when big fat rats, almost the size of a cat, invaded the village. It was said they carried plague, so whenever such a rat was spotted, women, men, and children, with sticks, would pursue it. The noise sometimes attracted workers in the fields who would join in the chase with whatever tool they held in hand. Caught, the rats became objects of fury. A few escaped. One in particular completely outsmarted hunters, traps and all. Even the cats seemed afraid of it. It would disappear into one house, or bush, only to reappear in another setting as if taunting humans. Or maybe they were many rats, shaped similarly. There was talk of witches inside the rat's body.

One day a man with a box with a trapdoor, all made of wire screen, appeared from nowhere. He had heard of the mysterious rat. He asked a few questions, and otherwise spoke few words. He hung something inside the box. He left the trap in one of the affected houses, and, lo and behold, the following day, when he came back, there was a big rat inside the box. The whole village followed the rat catcher, who disappeared as mysteriously as he had come. He did not ask for a reward. He never returned; and the rats, that size, did not reappear. Or so people claimed. Disagreements remained: Had it been just that one rat or many? The rat catcher became a legend.

I hope that as a mole catcher I can become as famous and have a grateful village follow me. But a mole catcher is not as glamorous as a rat catcher and nobody follows me except my younger brother. Moles can be elusive. A catcher needs a mix of skill, patience, and luck. The waiting is stressful, the pay meager and makes no dent in our needs.

There is the question of tuition particularly. My brother and I set out to do what we have always done: seek work at Lord Stanley Kahahu's farm, but now for tuition not wheels. Kahahu's estate and my grandfather's are separated by a hedge. Vast pyrethrum fields stand between our new home and our former homestead. I feel strange, joining my siblings in these same fields, coming as I now do from my grandfather's household. But the reunion with my other siblings, though only as workers in Kahahu's fields, goes quite well except for a sad awkwardness at evening time when we have to part and go our separate ways. Our earnings are not much. Besides, the work lasts for as long as there are flowers to pick, which means seven days or so.

Sometimes I accompany my mother when she goes to the Indian shops to look for work. Maybe I can also get something that pays more than what I get from picking pyrethrum and catching moles. The place has a different feel from that other time when she and I had gone to get my school uniform. Then my mind was focused on clothing stores. Now I pause at groceries: bags of beans, peas, sugar, and salt, and bins displaying packets of flour, green, red, and yellow peppers, garlic, onions, chiles, purslane, and fruits, papayas, mangoes, and dates. I also note the same picture of the frail Indian with eyeglasses, dressed in white trousers with a shawl flung over his shoulders, the one I had seen before. I now ask my mother who the man is and why his picture hangs on the walls of many shops. He is one of the Indian gods, she says without really paying much attention to the picture. Her mind is really set on getting work, any work, that will pay. Govji, in one of the shops, has a job for her: sorting potatoes. The good unblemished ones are put in sacks. The tiny ones are collected to be sold as seedlings. Damaged ones are thrown away. I help my mother. It is the most tedious thing I have ever done, more boringly repetitive than picking tea or pyrethrum. Catching moles and rats and building a store for trade are adventures, even though they don't pay. My enthusiasm wanes as days go by. But she needs the money to buy food she should not have had to buy and also for my tuition. She continues working at the potatoes without me. Sometimes she is allowed to take home some of the damaged potatoes as payment in kind.

There was an Indian shopkeeper named Manubhai but generally known as Manu. He spoke Gĩkũyũ fluently, though he sometimes mixed it up with Kiswahili. He had set up a bakery, Manubhai Limuru Bakery. His bread was also known as Manu as opposed to that baked in Elliot's Bakeries in Nairobi, which was simply referred to as Elliot. Manu and Elliot, as the loaves were named, were in competition. The Manu bakery produced more loaves than there were buyers, and sometimes he was forced to throw away piles of unsold bread in different stages of fermentation and decay. When this happened, word would quickly spread and many people, adults, children, women, and men, would descend upon the piles, and in no time every bit of bread would be gone. Once this coincided with our job hunt. I found myself among a horde grabbing at discarded bread and brought some home in triumph. Too bad Manubhai did not do this every day, and there was no way of telling when he next would.

I am becoming closer to my grandfather than I had been to my father. I am flattered when one day he asks that I go to his house. He sits on a finely carved three-legged stool. I sit on another, smaller one. Mũkami nourishes me with a glass of warm milk. Then he asks her to bring "the box." He takes out a bag from the box, dips into it, and comes up with a bunch of letters. Read that, he says, which I do. No, no, not that one, he would say, and I would go to the next, and so on until I got the right one. Yes, read it all, he says. He nods time and again as I read it. Hey! Hey! he exclaims with approval and delight. I am proud that my reading skills are recognized. Bring him some more tea, he calls out to his wife. Next he hands me paper and a pen, with ink. He dictates a reply word for word, line by line, paragraph by paragraph, asking me to go over what I had written till the letter has captured the tone he wants. Hey! Hey! he says, now laughing quietly in admiration and approval. "He can really hold a pen!" He raises his voice to his wife, who approaches with tea. He seems to be genuinely impressed with my learning. I become his scribe. He would often ask me to go to his house to help him write a letter but more often to read him old letters and help him sort out documents, including tax receipts. A headman at one time, he has developed a reverence for government-related papers. But he values any written documents and has bags of them in nice boxes. He would ask me questions about this or that document, what it said; then he would tell me how to arrange them. I have become his confidant though he never asks me for my opinion about the content. I am simply his personal scribe. In the process, I also get to eat nice food and drink tea with lots of milk. My grandfather has many cows. My mother likes this because it means one tummy less to feed. I get the impression that she and my grandfather's wife are not close.

My grandfather really loves his young wife Mũkami, who always wears Western-style dresses. She is completely devoted to his welfare. Though not haughty and certainly not given to fights with neighbors, she has an aloof bearing that keeps other women, even my mother, at a distance. Nobody would dare wander into her house without certain knowledge that they would be welcome. Sometimes I wonder if it was Mũkami who had driven Grandmother Gathoni away.

One evening Mũkami stops me outside Njango's hut. I should visit Grandfather first thing in the morning. I assume that he has a letter for me to read or write. But why so early in the morning? I am there, Mũkami opens the door, gives me a seat, and then my grandfather comes to the living room all dressed up. We share tea and sweet potato together. I wait for my assignment. Then my grandfather stands up, says farewell for the day, and leaves for some event out there. Mũkami says thank you to me and I leave, my mind puzzled but my tummy satisfied. Later in the evening Mũkami tells me that I should do the same the following morning.

Visiting my grandfather before any other visitor knocks at the door becomes part of my daily routine. I see it as some kind of privilege and savor the honor. It also makes me feel even closer to him. It is only later that I learn that I have merely replaced Gĩcini as the first caller at dawn. My grandfather believes that boys bring him good luck. He wants a boy to be his first encounter before a woman, any woman, even a girl, crosses his path. I am the new bird of good omen. Apparently good things happen to him after I visit him at dawn.

My grandfather must have been touched by the intolerable congestion and tension inside Njango's hut. Or maybe it is now clear that my father is not coming to plead for his wife and children. He sets aside a two-acre plot for my mother to put up a building, ironically next to Lord Kahahu's land.

My brother Wallace Mwangi, in the early stages as an apprentice carpenter, organizes the construction of a mud-walled, grass-thatched rondavel, almost a replica of the house we had left behind at my father's. Later he puts up his own, a four-cornered two-room house, resting on stilts. My sister, Njoki, whose marriage has gone awry, joins us. During the rainy season, my younger brother, my sister, and I decide to plant twigs of some bush all around the one-acre plot, in the hope that they will take root and form a hedge. The dry season arrives. My mother brings home a small twig of some tree and plants it just outside the courtyard. It is a pear tree, she says, and we laugh at her. Mother, you do things your own way; you don't plant it during the rains; you choose to do so when the rains are gone. She does not argue. She just smiles. But she waters it and by the end of the season our plantings have died, and the pear tree is alive. The hedge has to be done all over again.

And so new life begins: From a polygamous community we become a single-parent family. I continue playing my role as scribe and bird of good omen for my grandfather. But I will now be going to Manguo and back, from my new home with a lone pear tree just outside the courtyard.

School was about two miles from my new home, but still an improvement on the distance I used to cover when going to Kamandūra. It was midyear in grade three when I left Kamandūra school for Manguo school. Thinking that I was merely acting on my brother's advice, I was surprised to discover that I was part of an exodus, responding to the same pressures. It was not clear why I was really moving but I learned from other children that it had to do with two mysterious terms, "Kĩrore" and "Karĩng'a." Nobody explained what they meant or their origins. But they had a history.

After Kenya went from being British company property to being a colonial state in 1895, the state left education largely in the hands of Protestant and Roman Catholic missions, among them the Church Missionary Society, founded way back in 1799. Others such as the Gospel Missionary Society, founded in 1898, came after. The most prominent in my area was the Church of Scotland Mission, founded 1891, whose hub was in Thogoto, about twelve miles from Limuru, where, under Dr. J. W. Arthur, a school was established that was popularly known as Mambere, meaning "modern" or "progressive." The mission later opened outreach schools, like Kamandŭra, farther out. While these centers were influenced by modernity, *kĩrĩu*, and provided much-needed medical care and even taught useful skills in woodworking and agriculture alongside limited literary education, they were there to proselytize. Successful conversion was measured by how quickly, deeply, and thoroughly one divested oneself of one's culture and adopted new practices and values. For instance, among the Gĩkũyũ people, circumcision was considered a rite of passage marking the transition from youth, a stage of no legal accountability, to adulthood, with full responsibility. In 1929 a number of missionary societies in the Central Province—the Church of Scotland Mission led by Dr. Arthur; and the Gospel Missionary Society and the African Inland Mission, which had already condemned female circumcision as barbaric and unchristian—went further in their campaign against the practice and announced that all their African teachers and agents would have to sign a declaration solemnly swearing never to circumcise female children; never to become a member of the Kikuyu Central Association, the leading African political organization at the time; never to become a follower of Jomo Kenyatta, the KCA's general secretary, then in England as the organization's delegate; and never to join any party unless it was organized by the government or missionaries.* The declaration was asking the schools' Christian

---

* Theodore Natsoulas, "The Rise and Fall of the Kikuyu Karing'a Education Association of Kenya, 1929–1952," *Journal of African and Asian Studies* 23, nos. 3–4 (1988): 220–21, or go to http://jas.sagepub.com/cgi/content/abstract/23/3-4/219.

adherents to take a position against the practice and also the politics of resistance, which, despite the banning of Harry Thuku's East Africa Association in 1922, his exile and imprisonment, and the massacre of twenty-three Kenyans outside Nairobi's Central Police Station, had continued and even intensified under the KCA. There was a conflict of interests. From early on the missionaries had been the colonially accepted spokesmen for African interests, Dr. Arthur even having a seat in the colonial legislature as the official spokesman of African interests, whereas Europeans and Asians had their own direct representatives. So the struggle over female circumcision became a proxy for economics, politics, and culture and who and which organization had the right to speak for Kenyan Africans.

Kidole, the Swahili word for "thumbprint," became *kĩrore* in Gĩkũyũ and evolved into a pejorative term for those who signed or agreed to the declaration. Those who did not sign it, *aregi gũtheca kĩrore,* left the missionary institutions and joined the nascent African independent schools movement, followed, in most cases, by their students. One of the earliest known independent schools in Kenya was started in Nyanza by John Owalo, but in Central Province an independent elementary school was founded at Gĩthũngũri in 1925 by Musa Ndirangũ, a successful trader, and Wilson Gathuru, its first teacher, who also gave the land on which it was built. Initially a laborer on a white farm, Musa Ndirangũ went to school in 1911–1913 at a Gospel Missionary Society school in Kambũi, the home area of Harry Thuku. His attending school after his laboring days was in pursuit of personal independence, which he found in trade as his own boss. This mind-set was in tune with the politics of Harry Thuku, in part influenced by his ties to Marcus Garvey, whose slogan, Africa for the Africans, embodied the vision of self-reliance. Marcus Garvey had sought independence in business. Ndirangũ applied self-reliance by creating an elementary school run by Africans themselves. After the 1929 declaration, many other schools were founded by local committees of elders and teachers. Two organizations arose to oversee the development of the new schools. The Kikuyu Karĩng'a Education Association (KKEA) was launched in 1933 at Lironi, not far from Kamandũra, and the Kikuyu Independent Schools Association (KISA) in 1934 at Gĩtuamba, Mũrang'a.

The two organizations had religious affiliations: the African Independent Pentecostal Church for KISA and the African Orthodox Church for KKEA, with roots that went back to the American African Orthodox Church via South Africa through Bishop William Daniel Alexander, who visited Kenya for sixteen months between 1935 and 1937. The American African Orthodox Church had been formed by another Alexander, Bishop George Alexander McGuire, who earlier had been chief chaplain of Marcus Garvey's Universal Negro Improvement Association. "Karĩng'a" was the self-chosen term for orthodoxy in both tradition and religion. Christianity would be shorn of Western propensities, and tradition, of negative tendencies, the African being the judge of the shape and direction of change. Female circumcision was allowed but not required.

The terms "Kĩrore" and "Karĩng'a" became a way of characterizing the schools. Kĩrore, as applied to missionary schools, connoted schools that were deliberately depriving Africans of knowledge, in favor of training them to support the colonial state, which initially limited African education to carpentry, agriculture, and basic literacy only. Command of English was seen as unnecessary. The white settler community wanted "skilled" African labor, not learned African minds. Karĩng'a and KISA schools sought to break all limits to knowledge. The English language, seen as the key to modernity, also sparked contention. In government and missionary schools, the teaching of English started in grade four or later; in Karĩng'a and KISA schools, in grade three or even earlier, depending on the teachers.

So, in keeping with the traditions established by the educational wars of the time, Kamandũra was seen as denying us the kind of education that would propel us quickly into modern times. In contrast, Manguo was seen as having a more challenging curriculum, demanding rapid acquisition of English as we entered modern times.

Thus in moving from Kamandũra, a Kĩrore school, to Manguo, a Karĩng'a school, I was crossing a great historic divide that had begun way before I was born, and which, years later, I would still be trying to understand through my first novel, *The River Between*. But at the time I was not trying to understand history or act it out; I just wanted to realize my dreams of education in accordance with the pact that I had made with my mother.

English may have been cited as the prime reason for the exodus from Kamandũra to Manguo school, but I doubt if there was much difference in the teaching of the language. Nearly all the instructors were products of the mission and government schools and they could only draw on what they knew. In fact my own two teachers of English and history at Manguo, Fred Mbũgua and Stephen Thiro, were graduates of a Church of Scotland Mission school in Thogoto in Kikuyu, Dr. Arthur's missionary kingdom.

The difference lay in intangibles. When I think back on Kamandũra, what pops up are images of church, silent prayer, and individual achievement; in Manguo, images of performance, public spectacle, and a sense of community. Sunday services at Kamandũra had a set pattern: a text from the New Testament that carried the theme of the sermon of the day; prayers; and hymns that were Gĩkũyũ translations and renderings of the lyrics and melodies from the Church of Scotland Mission hymnbook. Without instrumental accompaniment, the melodies were slow, mournful, almost tired. The text, the hymns, and the sermon summoned calm introspection in older listeners, but impatience in the young. Manguo on Sunday was different.

Manguo, founded in 1928 on land given by the Kĩeya family, with Morris Kĩhang'ũ as the first head but later replaced by Fred Mbũgua and then Stephen Thiro, did not have a formal church building. On Sunday, the school hall became hallowed ground, the regular tables turned into a colorfully decorated altar and the regular benches into pews. The preacher on the first day that I attended was Morris Kĩhang'ũ, an ordinary teacher on weekdays, in the same school, not the most popular, prone as he was to using the stick to impose discipline and attentiveness in the class.

On the Sunday of my first attendance, I had never seen anything like this service. The hymns, often accompanied by drums and cymbals, had more zest and rhythm. Some were recent compositions, evoking contemporary events and experiences through biblical imagery. In fact many of the lyrics were based on biblical events. *In the times of hardship, O Lord, please don't turn your face away. When Daniel was put in the den of lions, Lord, you sent your angel . . .* etcetera. *When Cain pierced his brother Abel with a knife . . .* etcetera. *Samson and Delilah. David and Goliath.* What the Lord did then he could do now: give strength to the lowly and scatter their enemies.

The lines and the images in the various lyrics were familiar: I had read them in my copy of selections from the Old Testament, but from the lips of this mass of worshippers they carried a suggestion of sublime power. The soloists changed; any member of the congregation could join in, sometimes two taking over the next verse or repeating an earlier one. Some of the call-and-response was triadic: voices in unison, splitting into antiphony before coming together once more in triumphant reconciliation.

And then came the sermon; it was also based on a text from the Old Testament. The preacher started slowly, calmly, gradually raising his voice. Then would come dramatic changes in voice and gesture, as he sang, cajoled, pled, condemned, promised. He would tear off his shirt, baring his chest and beating it, acting out his humiliation, as he implored his God, the God of Isaac and Abraham, to do for the present people what he had done ages ago for the children of Israel, freeing them from oppression, leading them from slavery, across hot deserts, through roaring seas, blinding their pursuers. It was as if he had been an eyewitness to the exodus. Then he would assume the voice of God telling his followers: Tear up your hearts and not your clothes, and turn to me, for I am Jehovah your God! By this time the audience would be groaning and grunting assent, egging on their preacher. In the midst of the sermon, at an appropriate pause, or in response to an implied question, some member of the congregation would respond with a verse from a song, prompting the preacher and the congregation to join in, and then the preacher would resume his performance as if the response had been an integral part of the sermon. Seamlessly, Kĩhang'ũ is no longer the teacher I knew, his body and voice having changed. He is simultaneously conductor and mem-

ber of a vast orchestra. Yet when on Monday I see teacher
Kĩhang'ũ he looks so ordinary, frail even. Where is the voice
and the presence that I had seen make the ground move?

Though not always rising to the same intensity, performance permeated everything in Manguo, bespeaking a common experience and hope for collective deliverance. Success
and failure were not just personal: They included others. We
were competing not just among ourselves but also against
some other forces, even time. It was always one for all and all
for one.

Nothing showed this better than sports. Manguo did not
have good grounds or great sports facilities, but it made do
with what it had. One of my greatest thrills came from my
first attendance at a sports festival in a part of the Manguo
marshes that was often dry and firm in the hot season.

The festival started in the streets with a marching band,
which was new to me. The drum major, who wore a Scottish
kilt, guided the band with a baton decorated with green yarn
that ended in loose bobs and fluffs at both ends. Sometimes
he would throw the baton so high in the air that I gasped
with fear that he would not be able to catch it, but he always
did deftly without missing a step. The drums, the bugles,
and the trumpets seemed to be in conversation with each
other in beautiful wordless sounds.

As it wound its way through the market and shopping
centers, we children, even some adults, ran or tried to march
on either side of the band, to the entrance of the festival site
where only those with a ticket could enter. The grounds

were enclosed by a thick wall of grass and dry cornstalks so as to prevent mischievous efforts to create openings and peer through, efforts constantly thwarted by official watchful eyes, mostly of boys in scout uniforms. But there was little the organizers could do about those who sat atop the ridge or climbed up trees a distance away from the walls.

Within the grounds were sideshows, including a display of a little person whose words and antics were the subject of intense conversation afterward, but the major attractions included synchronized push-ups, leapfroging or jumping jacks, and tableaux, some of which, though made to look easy, seemed dangerous to me. Three-legged, egg-in-the-spoon, or human wheelbarrow races provoked raucous crowd involvement, but nothing could top the excitement generated by the athletic races, particularly the ones longer than a mile. Winners were heroes and heroines in their villages. As they ran the lap of honor, some in the crowd would join them. At the end of the day, an even bigger crowd followed the heroes and heroines all the way to their homes in triumph. Sometimes the crowd would carry them shoulder-high, the heroes or their helpers holding aloft the trophies won, be they basins, hoes, machetes, or axes, for prizes were always tools, not money.

The festival was an annual event among the Karĩng'a and KISA schools, which took turns hosting it, thus ensuring that it rotated from site to site, region to region. These events forged a togetherness between KISA and Karĩng'a while also tightening the bond between the schools and the community. The fact that the spectacles were organized without the colonial government or missionary help deepened the community's collective pride.

The sense of communal victory or loss was also felt in the classroom, much evident when the exam results were announced at the end of the year. Parents, guardians, relatives, and neighbors came to the school to participate in the celebration of excellence. It was a formal occasion attended by the school's founding elders, among them Mzee Kĩeya, who had donated the land, and whose son Stephen Thiro taught there. Whoever took the coveted three places, first, second, or third, was the pride of his family and community. Those who held the tail, as was the expression at the time, brought shame to their family. So every celebration of academic excellence was accompanied by laughter and tears, collective joy and grief. The pressure to do well must have produced the high degree of tolerance for corporal punishment, sometimes verging on abuse, that was so common in Manguo. The aggrieved children had no sympathy from their parents. The teacher was always right; after all, he was the daily eye of the community in the classroom.

Though things would change in years to come, I did not stand out in any subject during my first year at Manguo, not even in sports or physical education. But I had done something that caught the attention of Fred Mbũgua. I had written a class essay in Gĩkũyũ, a report on a meeting of an imaginary council of elders. He seemed to have been struck by the fact that I had captured the gravitas of elderly speech in my choice of words, imagery, and proverbs. The paper was read to the assembly. I can't remember if my elder brother was there. Certainly my mother was not. But by the time I reached home, my mother knew about it. That I had been made to stand up and take a bow was confirmation of my having done the best I could.

My mother must have been pleased, because later she allowed me to climb up her dear pear tree and shake down some fruit. She guarded it jealously with love and care, and the tree, as if returning the favor, often bore a lot of fruit.

I was happy that my class exercise had made her happy and had brought collective honor and pride to my new community.

I did not know that I would soon become a traveling troubadour. Music at Kamandūra accompanied religious ceremony, prayer mostly; at Manguo music was incorporated in
everything, secular and religious. Even the sports festival
had choirs who marked the intermissions, an alternative
to the marching band. Performances, including music and
dance, were part of the year-end school assemblies. Some of
these were simple skits and sketches.

Two made an impression on me for a long time. One,
called "a bicycle built for two," was the story of a love trian-
gle wherein two male friends outwit each other to win the
love of a girl. They end up fighting, giving the girl an opportunity to slip away. Both lose. The other had something to do
with justice or the art of righting wrongs unjustly. A mother
has left two bananas for her two children to share. The two
brothers start fighting over the bananas; both want the bigger one. An old man, looking every inch a caring adult,
passes by, sees the problem, and offers to help by making the
two bananas equal. Taking both pieces of fruit in his hands,
he compares them and bites a piece off the bigger one, only
to create a new inequality, which he tries to rectify in the

same way. Eventually he finishes off both bananas, leaving the brothers to ponder the equality of loss. Too late the brothers join forces against the old man, who runs off the stage as if the bananas have given him new youth. The skits were all in mime yet they were so eloquent, they generated applause, laughter, and nods of understanding.

The performance of songs, most of which had educational themes, produced a different mood and made some in the assembly tear up.

Korwo nĩ Ndemi na Mathathi
Baba ndagwĩtia kĩrugũ
Njoke ngwĩtie itimũ na ng'ombe,
Rĩu baba, ngũgwĩtia gĩthomo

Ndegwa rĩu gũtitũire
Thenge rĩu no iranyihahanyiha
Ndirĩ kĩrugũ ngũgwĩtia
Rĩu baba, ngũgwĩtia gĩthomo

If these were the times of our ancestors Ndemi and
   Mathathi
My father, I would ask you for the feast due to initiates,
Then I would ask you to arm me with a spear and shield,
But today, Father, I ask you for education only

Our herd of bulls is gone
Our he-goats depleted
I will not ask you for a banquet
My father, all I ask for is education

There were other variations in which the singers asked for writing materials, pen and slate, instead of spear and shield. I took the lyrics and melody personally: I felt as if they were expressing the fate of my father's herds.

Gradually the new songs spread beyond the school, sparked by an emerging social trend among young men and women. On Sunday afternoons they would arrange social gatherings in homes or in the open air where they would converse and sing. The railway station platform was no longer the main social center. It was at such a gathering in my new home that I first sang the Ndemi Mathathi song, at the playful urging of the young men and women in my brother Wallace's place. The emotion I put into the singing came from a heart soaked with recent loss: the depletion of my father's cattle, my expulsion from home. The public and private emotion of loss intersected. The crowd joined in the singing. My rendering had captured, in ways that I had not expected, the mood of the hour.

My brother Wallace decided that I was a singer. Wherever there was a gathering of young men and women he would find a way of making sure that I displayed my talent. Being small for my age, I always aroused curiosity. The results were always the same: adult involvement, adulation afterward. The boy is smart. The boy who wrote the essay that Mwa-limu, Fred Mbũgua read at assembly was also a singer.

I was now in my second year at Manguo. I had already completed the Competitive Entrance Exam at grade four and passed well. It was a terminal exam, a real hurdle in the competition for school. The exam was later abolished: So many kids would fail, ending their education; they would become workers for the tea and coffee plantations. Passing the exam added to my reputation among my brother Wallace's friends.

One morning I arrived at the school earlier than I normally did and found a group of students singing instead of playing as they usually did before the morning assembly. I was transfixed. The melody was familiar: Where had I heard it?

Then I remembered. One day while still in my father's house I had gone down to the Manguo marshes. During the rainy season the marshes were, of course, soggy and remained so for many months, sometimes even until the next rainy season. Reeds grew. Birds flew above the marsh; some made their nests among the grass and reeds where they laid eggs. There was a dirt road that joined Limuru to the Nairobi–Nakuru Road built by the Italian prisoners of war. Some white people used to come there to shoot birds, their dogs thrashing in the water to retrieve the fallen game. I had not even crossed the road when, at a place we used to call Kĩmunya's corner, I saw a convoy of trucks with men and women caged in the back.

Any convoy of trucks along this road always brought back the memory of the accident in the murram quarry that killed army men and wounded others during the Second World War. My tummy would tighten up, fearful of another accident. The convoy that I saw produced the same fears. There was no accident, but the people sang as if they had witnessed or expected one.

I did not catch all the words, but the melody and the way they sang it, with total conviction, touched me with its defiance and immeasurable sadness. I would have liked to know the words.

And now these students were singing the lyrics!

Wendani ndonire kuo
Wa ciana na atumia
Mboco yagwa thĩ tũkenyũrana
Hoyai ma, thai thai Ma
Amu Ngai no ũrĩa wa tene

Great love I saw there
Among women and children
When a morsel was picked from the ground
It was shared equally among us
Pray to him fervently
Beseech him fervently
He is the God eternal

The same words, the same melody, as if the students had been part of the convoy of the caged. I learned the verse and the chorus and added it to my repertoire. I needed only to start singing and grown-ups would take it up.

My singing made some of my brother's friends, who often came to visit him in his new single-bedroom house, start talking to me about affairs of the land as if I myself was a grown-up. They nicknamed me Mzee, "Elder," a term of respect. I called them Mzee in turn. They were adults, my elder brother's peers, but Mzee became a nickname among us. The most learned and knowledgeable in the adult group was Ngandi Njũgũna.

"It is the song of Ole Ngurueni," Ngandi explained to me when I asked him about its popularity.

"Ole Ngurueni?" I asked, puzzled.

"From 1902 onward when Europeans stole our lands they turned many of the original owners into squatters by force, or guile, or both. You see, to get money for taxes one had to work for pay, somewhere. Then after the First World War more Africans had their lands taken from them to make way for soldier settlement. Some of them went to the Rift Valley, increasing the squatter population. Then in 1941, even as our men went to fight for them in the big war, European settlers started expelling squatters from their farms, displacement a second time. Ole Ngurueni, near Nakuru, was a resettlement area for some of those who had been displaced. But then, three years after the return of our soldiers from the Second World War, the colonial government decided to expel the residents of Ole Ngurueni, yet again, a third time. The dwellers of Ole Ngurueni made a stand: They would not move; they would not be moved from their homes three times. Their power? Solidarity. They swore to stick together and never break ranks. The family of one of the leaders, Koina, comes from Limuru. What did the government do? Placed them in trucks, like cattle, brought them to Yatta in Eastern Kenya. They put the narrative of their forced removal from Ole Ngurueni to Yatta, a region they called the land of black rocks, into song."

It was in 1948 that I first heard the song. I did not know

that two, three years later I would hear it again at Manguo or that I would be singing it to a very responsive crowd, some of whom may have been relatives of the victims.

According to Ngandi, Ole Ngurueni, a tale of displacement, exile, and loss, was really a story of Kenya; people's resistance was a harbinger of things to come.

Ngandi was educated and trained as a teacher at the Kenya
Teachers' College at Gĩthũngũri. He talked about his alma
mater with pride: It offered the best education in the world.

The college was a product of the competition for teachers
and students between the alliance of KISA and KKEA
on the one hand and the Kĩrore and Thirikari, the state
and the missionary programs, on the other. Even after the
growth of independent African schools intensified starting
in 1929, the government and mission centers remained the
source of trained teachers, and they were reluctant to admit those candidates who came directly from the two independent organizations, KISA and KKEA. The independent
schools continued poaching teachers from the missionary
centers, meeting the shortage with the untrained. Yet both
KISA and Karĩng'a prided themselves on being beyond government and missionary control. The quest for self-reliance
with respect to teachers was the challenge that led to the
conception of a Kenya Teachers' College at Gĩthũngũri, the
site of the first independent elementary school founded by
Musa Ndirangũ. The site symbolized continuity.

The mind behind the conception and the execution of

this teachers' college was Mbiyũ Koinange, the first son of the legendary Senior Chief Koinange. After a stint at Alliance High School in Kikuyu, Mbiyũ went to Virginia's Hampton Institute in 1927 for his secondary school education, the same school from which a famous African American educator, Booker T. Washington, had graduated in 1875 and where he taught before going on to start Tuskegee Institute in Alabama in 1881 at the recommendation of General Armstrong, the principal of the Hampton Institute. Mbiyũ must have carried himself well to have elicited, on his graduation from Hampton, appreciative comments from fellow students: A noble person goes his way, conscious of his nobility, they said of him.

After Hampton, Mbiyũ went to Ohio Wesleyan College, graduating with a B.A. in 1935. His graduation from Ohio drew the attention of *Time*, in the issue dated June 4, 1935, which listed Negro spirituals as among his interests. Describing him as the son of a dancer, it noted his eagerness to return home to promote "yearning for learning" in his community, whose members' otherwise "prime ambition," the issue editorialized, "is to make his earlobes touch his shoulders." *Time* had obviously never heard of Harry Thuku and his anticolonial workers' movement of the 1920s, or the struggle for education led by those very long lobed elders. Mbiyũ went on to Columbia University, for his master's in education, the first Kenyan African to acquire a higher degree. Returning to Kenya in 1938 and in consultation with his father, he came up with a solution: an African-run, community-owned college, modeled on Hampton and Tuskegee, and he would be the principal. With its dreamers hoping that it would eventually develop into Kenya University, the college was to become one of the biggest and most ambitious educational projects ever undertaken in colonial Kenya. In modeling itself on Hampton and Tuskegee, the college was reconnecting itself to the Garveyite concepts of self-reliance that, through Harry Thuku and the *Negro World*, had inspired the start of the independent schools. Garvey had himself been attracted to the Tuskegee model when in 1914 he left Jamaica for the USA, but he arrived too late to meet with Washington, who died in 1915.

The Kenyan dreamers looked to their cultural traditions for solutions to funding problems, ironically based on the contentious practice of circumcision. Every Gĩkũyũ adult, man or woman, belonged to an age set, based on the year they were initiated. Money would be raised through age groups, each competing with others to see which could raise the most. But there were other individual initiatives and innovations.

The story is told of one illiterate peasant woman, Njeri, who went to see the famed college for herself. She was horrified to find that while the boys lived in rooms built with stones, the girls slept in a hut of mud walls and grass thatch. She went back to her village and started organizing women, who gave whatever they could afford toward buying stones and aluminum for the girls' dorm. Her initiative became a woman's movement expanding beyond her village.

The effort to raise money mobilized the entire adult Gĩkũyũ community, and the Kenya Teachers' College at

Gĩthũngũri became part of the collective pride enshrined in many popular songs of the time.

> When you get to Gĩthũngũri
> You'll find an African people's college
> It's a four-story building
>
> The builders are Kenyans
> The overseer is a Kenyan
> The committee is made up of Kenyans

The college, which also incorporated secondary schooling, was thus seen as a counterweight to the colonial and missionary project, which always assumed the fragility of the African mind. Open to all Kenyan Africans, Kenya Teachers' College at Gĩthũngũri was an institution committed to producing teachers who would provide African children with unlimited, unbiased knowledge, enabling them to compete with the best that the government and missionary schools offered. The college inspired intellectuals organically connected to the community, who would be traveling interpreters of the world to the people.

Ngandi Njũgũna was of that ambition and tradition. He always talked about the day the college was formally opened on January 7, 1939, as a great day for Kenya. Though it opened at a time of war, it survived the hardships. He claimed that even many Europeans and Asians used to visit the college to witness the initiative for themselves. Black American soldiers stationed in Nairobi visited the college and even sang Negro spirituals for the community. Ngandi could never talk for long about anything without somehow bringing the Kenya Teachers' College into the conversation.

He first stood out from the crowd around me when he lent me a book that soon became second only to my torn copy of the Old Testament as most prized. It was *Mwendwo nĩ Irĩ na Irĩri* (*Beloved of the People*), written by Justus Itotia, a teacher at Jeans School, at Kabete near Nairobi, founded in 1925 for rural community development. The book was a collection of essays, riddles, and stories all promoting the ideal of a good person whose moral character was molded by the values of civility, responsibility, and mutual accountability, which, though found in the old culture, anticipate and find fulfillment in the Christian ideals of the modern world. Two narratives were exemplary: a parable and a prosaic description of a journey.

A man about to go to trade in another country asks his friend, a herdsman, to look after his black-and-gray-spotted cows while he is away. The cow gives birth at about the same time as the herdsman's brown cow. Since the spotted cow is known for high yield in milk, the herdsman simply exchanges the calves, giving the spotted one to the brown mother to suck and the brown one to the spotted mother. Eventually the man returns to claim his cow and its offspring only to find the oddity of a spotted calf being mothered by the brown cow and the brown calf by the spotted mother. Realizing what has happened, he takes the matter to the elders. Though the elders suspect the truth because of the color of the calves, they cannot come to a consensus because it is one person's word against another's. Out of pity for the suffering of the council of elders, for the case dragged on for years with the disputed calves giving birth to others who gave birth to still others, a boy offers to settle the case. The elders are skeptical, but since they are at their wits' end, they let him try. They follow his instructions. On the eve of the next session, they secretly put him in a hole and, leaving enough room for air, they cover it with a rock that tested their combined strength in rolling it to the place. When the man and the herdsman come for the hearing, the elders, who are seated very far from the rock, first ask the herdsman to go and bring the rock to the elders. Failing, after much sweat and toil, and seeing that he is all alone, he mutters to himself, Why on earth did I ever exchange the calves, instead of holding on to what is mine? He goes back to the elders. The other complainant is given the same instructions. Failing to move the rock even an inch, he mutters to himself: However hard the task, I will never give up on what is rightfully mine. The entire court now moves and sits all around the rock as if before an oracle. The voice from the rock tells them what each of the men has said, and the case is settled and justice is done. In the character of the fictional boy who grows up to become the wisest man of his times are hints of a precocious Jesus or Solomon figure.

The other narrative is a description of a school trip to the Ondiri marshes in Kikuyu. Nothing really happens: Students gather at the school compound, they walk, they arrive, they eat, and they go back. But we can learn about the values that are praised: cleanliness, punctuality, cooperation, good manners, aspects of the new African and the new Christian civics.

I did not know where the Ondiri marshes were, but I liked to think of them as a magical place. Otherwise why devote pages to a journey during which nothing really happens, in which there were no twists and turns? But although the book did not lift me to the heights that the Old Testament had taken me, it had the immediate appeal of talking about things around me. The book taught me that one could write about the commonplace and still make it interesting.

A vast reservoir of general knowledge, Ngandi always carried a newspaper, mostly *Mũmenyereri*, the popular Gĩkũyũ-language weekly edited by Henry Muoria, well folded and placed inside the outer pocket of his jacket. He would read bits from it to his listeners to make a point, but mostly he just referred to it. He was a kind of itinerant scholar, unfolding his book of vast knowledge wherever he found two or three gathered together.

His knowledge extended to songs and he added to my repertoire. His favorite was *Come my friend, let's reason together. For the sake of the future of our children. May darkness in our country end.* He sang it in a tremulous voice, which I could not re-create, a sad strain below the words, but he seemed proud when his pupil displayed what he had taught him no matter the quality of the singing. I was his discovery. He liked introducing me at some gatherings, dramatizing the fact that on top of singing I could read the Bible, *Mũmenyereri*, and *Mwendwo nĩ Irĩ na Irĩri* fluently.

I don't know when or how it happened but I came to realize that the adults were prolonging the duration of the songs I initiated by adding many more verses to them. They would sing a song over and over and then move to other songs. I was merely a trigger. In time, themes other than purely educational ones crept into the songs, as did names like Waiyaki wa Hinga, Mbiyũ Koinange, Jomo Kenyatta.

Njamba ĩrĩa nene Kenyatta
Rĩu nĩ oimire Rũraya
Jomo nĩ oimĩte na thome
Ningĩ Jomo mũthigani witũ

Kenyatta our great hero
Has now returned from Europe.
He came back through the main gate (Mombasa).
Jomo has been our eyes.

Ngandi would often add background information about historical figures and incidents, mentioned as if he knew them personally or had been present when certain things happened in Africa, Europe, and America. He even talked about characters in the grave, Waiyaki, for instance. Waiyaki wa Hinga was the paramount leader of the Gĩkũyũ of southern Kiambu when Europeans arrived at Dagoretti in 1887. In 1890 he welcomed Captain Lugard in Dagoretti, where they took a solemn oath of brotherhood between the two peoples. Lugard's followers broke the oath, built Fort Smith, and made it clear, in their hostile actions, that they had come to conquer. Waiyaki mounted the resistance of the spear against the gun but the gun won; he was captured and buried alive at Kibwezi. If you had heard Ngandi talk about Wai-yaki's fate, you would believe that he had been there to hear Waiyaki's last defiant announcement that he would come back in the spirit of his people to haunt the whites till they left Kenya. Waiyaki's last wish in 1891, the call to arms in defense of the land, was Ngandi's first article of political and legal faith. The other was the Devonshire declaration of 1923 that Kenya was an African people's country and the interests of the African natives had to be paramount. The declaration was an acknowledgment of the rightness of Wai-yaki's last words, Ngandi would say, hinting that Waiyaki was a prophet. Ngandi had a way of introducing debates and igniting discussions on themes that ranged from land, education, and religion to the personalities of Mbiyũ Koinange and Jomo Kenyatta. Ngandi often saw the hand of fate in numbers, coincidences, and even dates: For instance, the fact that both men went abroad within a year of each other, Mbiyũ to America in 1927 and Kenyatta to England in 1929, was a clear sign that their paths would cross.

Kenyatta had gone abroad before I was born, sent to be the voice of the Kikuyu Central Association. The KCA, though the successor to Harry Thuku's East African Association, could only register as a regional body, because the colonial state was no longer allowing any countrywide African organization. Kenyatta had come back briefly before returning to England in 1931, where he stayed for fifteen years representing KCA even though it was banned in 1941 in his absence. Along the way he had become a nationalist and a Pan-Africanist. He had told the British in their own country: Kenya is an African peoples' country, bequeathed to us by our ancestors, and nobody can take it away from us. Upon disembarking from the boat in Mombasa in 1946, he bent down and held a fistful of Kenyan soil close to his chest; it was the stuff of legends. He had written the book *Facing Mount Kenya* and another, *Kenya: The Land of Conflict*.

As for Mbiyũ, he was not just educated; he was the most learned in the world, some insisted. People claimed that when he spoke English, even the owners of the language had to consult a dictionary. The two learned giants were rivals. No, the two giants were bosom friends: Kenyatta had even married Mbiyũ's sister. But had Kenyatta not married an English woman in England? So many stories, so many myths.

Ngandi, who claimed that he had read *Kenya: The Land of Conflict*, tried to make sense of all this to his circle of admirers. But even he seemed conflicted as to who was the greater. Kenyatta had wisdom given to him by birth; Mbiyũ had knowledge given to him by books. Wisdom was a gift from God and learning a gift from man, and that was why Mbiyũ always deferred to Kenyatta. See? Mbiyũ is the founder of the Kenya Teachers' College, but when Kenyatta comes back from England in 1946, what does Mbiyũ do? Makes Kenyatta the principal. The whole self-reliance thing, that is Mbiyũ. He has the mind, the hand, but not the voice. Jomo has the mind, the voice, but not the hand. Look, a big struggle is always led by a pair: Gandhi and Nehru; Mao and Chou En-lai. Moses and Aaron. The hand of genius and the voice of genius. Without one, there is not the other. Mbiyũ and Kenyatta had survived the Second World War, and there was a reason that fate had arranged that they return to the land, one of them just before the beginning of the war, and the other, soon after the war. It was to lead Kenya from slavery to the promised land. The journey to the promised land was not easy; it was full of trials and tribulations, tears, even blood!

The suffering of Ole Ngurueni was part of a pattern. It was Ngandi, through his talks of the squatters' resistance and other tales, imagined or culled from newspapers, who conveyed and reinforced in me the sense that something unusual, something of biblical proportions, was stirring in the land. But one could also feel it through whispers of happenings and hints of others to come, with Nairobi at the center. Fact and rumor generated more fact and rumor in quick succession. Most dramatic was the new rumor that all workers in Kenya had come together under the umbrella of the East African Trade Union Congress; that they had called a general strike to oppose the granting of a royal charter to Nairobi, in 1950, which raised its status from a municipality to a city. The word "city" became ominous, evil, threatening. How would Nairobi the city be different from Nairobi the town that my father once ran away from: the Nairobi whence army trucks had come to crash into my mother's house; the Nairobi where my mother and I had walked after my eyes were healed at King George VI Hospital?

The royal charter would mean that Africans would be removed from the town, and from areas surrounding Nairobi, as had happened to black people in South Africa, explained Ngandi coolly. Remember that the Kenya Boers came here from South Africa. They expelled the dwellers of Ole Ngurueni in 1948 even as Boers in South Africa were doing the same to black people. White people had a master plan to make Africa, from Cape to Cairo, their own. It was Cecil Rhodes, owner of stolen diamonds and gold in South Africa, who had originally hatched the evil scheme. Ngandi elaborated. In the 1930s there was a secret society of whites based in Kenya plotting to kill black babies at birth, save a few strong in body for labor but feeble in mind and unable to plot resistance. It was called the Eugenics Society (Kiama Kia Njini), which in my imagination registered as a society of white arsonists, man-eating ogres, the kind that Kabae and others had gone to fight in the Second World War. And now this royal charter to clear black people from the city and the remaining lands contrary to Ngandi's beloved 1923 Devonshire declaration! The white race was against the black race although he, Ngandi, made exceptions for people like Fenner Brockway, a Labor Forty member of the British parliament. Otherwise Ngandi's narrative drew a picture of an encroaching reptilian white evil threatening to swallow us all. But battling this white master plan in the shadows of history were young men, some of whom had already confronted white men during the war and triumphed over them, although on behalf of the British. In the spirit of Waiyaki, they were now standing up for Kenya and Africa. The struggle against the white master plan was encapsulated in the fight now unfolding against the royal charter. There had been the great Mombasa strike in 1947, Ngandi explained, but the current battle in the streets of Nairobi in 1950, after the workers had gone on strike, again was more reminiscent of the struggle during the times of Harry Thuku in 1922, which had resulted in the Devonshire declaration, suggesting that an even more momentous declaration might emerge from this struggle. Then, in 1922, as now, in 1950, the rural folk supplied food to the strikers and welcomed to their homes those workers who escaped the brutality of the government forces.

Some of those who took part in the 1950 strike against the royal charter were from Limuru and brought with them new whispers and rumors about Bildad Kaggia, Fred Kubai, Chege Kibachia, George Ndegwa, Achieng Oneko, Dedan Mugo, and Paul Ngei, among others. The names occupied a space between the real and the unreal, history and story, and I added them to my pantheon of mythical heroes. But the young men and women who told of the turmoil in the streets of Nairobi were real flesh and blood: They seemed serious and purposeful in their words and demeanor. I was a willing recipient of their tales of daring and narrow escapes, triumph and disaster, bespeaking a will hardened by woe. Yes, Waiyaki lived on.

I started interpreting events and anecdotes biblically. There was a story about an Indian prophet who had returned to Kenya and appeared before a multitude in Kaloleni Hall to say that it was time for white people to go and leave Africans to rule themselves. He had been arrested and in front of the judge said the same thing: Africans can rule themselves. Words never before spoken so directly. His name was Makhan Singh. Apparently this was not his first time in Kenya; every time he came into the country his words would make something big happen, strikes mostly. Ngandi went so far as to claim that Singh started his prophecies as a thirteen-year-old, having just arrived in Nairobi in 1927, the same year that young Mbiyũ had left for America. The colonial government would ban him, deport him to India, but time and again he sneaked back. But this time, his place of birth had mysteriously disappeared, one part of it becoming India and the other Pakistan, and neither country would accept such a dangerous prophet among its people. Governor Philip Mitchell, with orders from London, had him whisked from the courtroom and banished to the desert, where his voice could not be heard. But Singh would surely reappear and then something momentous would happen, as it had before, as evidenced by the strikes. There were whispers of a land movement that would bring about the fulfillment of his prophecy. And then in August 1950 the government announced that a secret movement called Mau Mau had been banned.

In my mind, and because their names were everywhere in the songs we sang, I connected the genius pair of Koinange and Kenyatta with everything that was happening in the country: the Indian man's prophecy, especially after Ngandi pointed out the strange coincidence of the arrival of the child-prophet in 1927 and the departure of Mbiyũ for America the same year; the Ole Ngurueni women who sang that, on their arrival in Yatta, they had received a telegram from Kenyatta in Gĩthũngũri inquiring if they had arrived safely; the striking workers in many parts of the country and now the secret movement. In my imagination the Kenyatta and Koinange of the songs and of Ngandi's talks became fictional characters, larger than life. I imagined a million Kenyan eyes on a giant Kenyatta's face. I longed to meet the pair, the way one hopes that one may come across a favorite fictional character in real life but knowing full well that such an encounter is impossible.

I was lucky with Mbiyũ. My eldest sister, Gathoni, was married to Kĩariĩ, who had lost his job at the Limuru Bata Shoe factory after the 1947 strike. They lived in Kĩambaa, next to the land owned by the legendary Senior Chief Koinange. Kĩariĩ's father looked after Koinange's extensive orchard of plums and pears. My younger brother and I used to visit our sister to babysit her first child, Wanjirũ. My sister's house was also very close to that of Charles Karũga Koinange, Mbiyũ's younger brother. Karũga's wife, Nduta, and Gathoni, my sister, were on visiting terms, and that was how I first met Wilfred and Wanduga, sons of Charles Karũga Koinange. Wilfred and I were in the same grade, though in different schools in different regions. He and I loved school. So we had plenty in common. Years later, in the early 1960s, I would meet him at Makerere University College, Kampala, where he studied medicine, and I, English. But at the time of our youth and despite our budding friendship he did not have what I wanted: the power and the brilliance to conjure up Mbiyũ from the realm of fiction.

And then an opportunity presented itself. My younger brother and I were at my sister's at the same time. We were walking on a narrow path with hedges on either side behind which was a thick growth of green corn when we heard two women talking and pointing to a person going in the same direction but ahead of us. That's him, they said. The son of Koinange, Mbiyũ himself. He was probably going home after a visit with his brother Charles, or he may have been taking a walk around his father's enormous estate. This was our chance, I told my younger brother, who was not as obsessed as I was with a person in a gray suit walking pensively along a rural path away from us. But he was always game when it came to adventure. Let's make sure. Let's greet him. Taking courage from each other, we dashed behind a hedge and ran through the cornfields. Making sure that we had gone past him, we emerged from the hedges onto the path, walking toward him. How are you, Mbiyũ wa Koinange, we called out in unison. He seemed a little taken aback, and then said, I am well. We did not wait for more. We ran, shouting, Yes, it's him. But I was a little disappointed. He seemed a less imposing figure than the Mbiyũ of my imagination and Ngandi's description. The mind can play tricks; months later in 1951 I heard of songs sung by Kenya African Union (KAU) crowds at Kaloleni Hall, Nairobi, as they sent Mbiyũ and Achieng Oneko to England to air grievances, the Mbiyũ of the imagination was back, so different from the one I had seen walking that day.

Perhaps the real Kenyatta, whenever and wherever I might meet him, would match the Kenyatta of legends. But his home was far away in Gatũndũ and I did not have relatives married in the region. It was unlikely that I would ever be in a position to catch him in a gray suit walking alone, pensively, on a country path through green cornfields.

Then I heard from Ngandi, who seemed to know everything, that Jomo Kenyatta would be coming to Limuru. He did not know the day, the week, or the month. But I was sure of one thing: I was not about to let the chance pass me by. I did not tell anybody. I simply started frequenting my elder brother's furniture store at the Limuru African marketplace.

Wallace Mwangi, or Good Wallace as he was becoming known, was my mother's first major success. He was born in 1930 and later went to Manguo school for a few years beginning in 1945. He had interesting study habits, especially before a test: He would work all night, with an open paraffin lantern, feet in a basin of cold water to keep him awake, but I suspect that the lack of sleep was not very conducive to good performance. He would try to sell his theory and practice to anybody who would listen. He did not persuade me. With my past history of bad eyes, I disliked the very thought of studying all night by an oil lamp with my feet in cold water, but he never gave up selling the idea. My mother, who paid his tuition, did not interfere with his school efforts except once when he announced that he intended to become a boy scout. In Gĩkũyũ, the word "scout" sounded like *thikauti*, or *thika hiti*, to my mother, and somebody must have confirmed her worst fears that my brother would become a "burier of dead hyenas." She pleaded with him, she threatened, and she did not want to hear an explanation. She just could not imagine her son becoming a professional mourner and burier of dead hyenas. I doubt if any other animal would have been more tolerable to her, but the hyena was the worst character in stories: greedy, dirty, and it fed on the remains of humans. I don't know if it was because he caved in to her concerns or because he left school afterward, but he never became a boy scout.

This may have left, in my brother, a desire that he fulfilled vicariously through the lady with whom he fell in love and eventually married. Charity Wanjikŭ was born in 1935 in Kĭmuga village, Kĭambaa, next to my sister Gathoni's place and Charles Koinange's. She went to Kĭambaa Church Missionary Society school, where she joined the girl guides squad. Even when not in uniform, Charity often wore a blue beret, leaving all the young men of Limuru agog with envy and admiration. Wallace got himself a girl guide, they would whisper or even say loudly. They nicknamed her Rendi ya Banana, "Lady from Banana Hills," because the banana place, being on the highway between Nairobi and Limuru, was better known and sounded more esoteric than Kĭmuga or Kĭambaa, which sounded like villages next door. That was years later, of course, in 1954, and my mother had no objections to having a girl guide for a daughter-in-law because the name did not sound like "boy scout."

Now, relieved and even grateful that her son had heeded her concerns, my mother funded his other dreams, time and again selling he-goats she may have been fattening, or black wattle trees she had grown on one of her parcels of land.

After leaving school he joined Kabae's legal and secretarial services as an apprentice typist. His English would not have created great demand for his secretarial skills, but whatever he did, he would add a little something. He tried his hand at making a wooden typewriter that he claimed would be faster and less noisy than Kabae's Remington. He abandoned both projects and became apprenticed to a carpenter, Joseph Njoroge, about his age. Such an apprenticeship was supposed to last several years, but after only a few months my brother had started making his own things on the side. Here his creative talents and persuasive skills came together, and soon he had more customers than the master carpenter. He did something no African artisan from the area had done. He rented the backyard of an Indian shop owned by Govji, or Ngũnji in its Gĩkũyũnized form, where he made and displayed beds and chairs, competing with the more skilled and experienced Indian artisans. His business kept on expanding, and he rented a much bigger yard, halfway between the Indian and African shops. The space belonged to Karabu, who was in the transport business, and who had lost one of his legs in a road accident. By this time Good Wallace was even hiring the occasional services of Joseph Njoroge, the master carpenter. The owner of the premises resented my brother's success and tried to force him out by raising the rent very steeply. He eventually did get him out by claiming he needed the space for his own use. My brother ended up renting a building in the Limuru marketplace, where he set up his workshop and furniture store.

Among his own apprentices was Kahanya wa Njue, one of his closest friends, whose elder brother, Karanja the driver, or simply Ndereba as he was known, had married my half sister Nyagaki, Gacoki's third born. Kahanya had also been to Manguo school, but dropped out after beating up the teacher Wahinya, who was much younger than him, and who had tried to discipline him. Unlike other apprentices who paid to learn, Kahanya was paid for his work. He and my brother Wallace were social friends, literally inseparable. They moved to the new premises together, and Kahanya eventually became his assistant, although he was never nearly as good as the master carpenter Njoroge.

I had frequently visited my brother's workshop when it used to be at the Indian shops and Karabu's place, but not with the regularity that I did now that I was looking for the opportunity to meet Kenyatta. Manguo school was not far from the marketplace, and at lunch breaks I would run there and back in time for afternoon classes. The marketplace thrived with artisans of all kinds: shoemakers; bicycle repairers and motor vehicle mechanics; makers of aluminium utensils, charcoal burners, and other household gadgets; and tailors with noisy Singer sewing machines.

Like the Bata Shoe factory workers, who often visited our home with an eye on the girls, so did the members of the artisan class. With their independent self-employed base, they were a social notch above the working class as eligible bachelors. That was how the humorous shoemaker and flamboyant dancer Gatanjeru son of Mariu captured the heart of my half sister Minneh Wanjirũ wa Gacoki; Mr. Washerman Wanjohi, that of beautiful Mũmbi, Baba Mũkũrũ's daughter; and the religious tailor, Willie Ng'ang'a, that of another half sister, the equally religious Wambũkũ wa Njeri, edging out a large crowd of suitors. But the workers, including those employed in the restaurants and butcher shops in the marketplace, attracted their fair share of fluttering hearts.

At one of the corners was Kĩmũchũ's shop and restaurant. Uncle Kĩmũchũ was the oldest son of one of the women my grandfather had inherited upon the death of his relative Ndũng'ũ. Uncle Gĩcini, who had now left Kamandũra, worked there.

Now and then Good Wallace would give me a few cents. I would run down to Uncle Kĩmũchũ's restaurant to buy *mandazi*, or *matumbuya*, as we called them, a kind of deep-fried dough, often fresh from the cooking oil. Kĩmũchũ's was a very popular eating place. There was a pile of *Mũmenyereri* newspapers but no seller in sight. People just picked up their copy and put down the right amount or took the right amount of change. Kĩmũchũ himself, obese, light-skinned, was nearly always behind the counter at his shop next door, and I got the impression that he did not know who I was because he never nodded recognition at me.

I enjoyed those days of waiting for Kenyatta at my brother's workshop. I came to like the smell of wood, unvarnished or varnished. I liked shuffling through the wood shavings and the sawdust on the floor. I came to appreciate the muscular and imaginative demands of woodworking. I noted how meticulous my brother was with everything: designs and finishes. He would work on something, and just when I was sure he was done I would see him go at it over and over again till it achieved the refinement he wanted. Whatever he made was unique. He tried to inculcate his work ethic in his employees, including his friend and assistant Kahanya, but they were not so patient. He persisted, impressing upon them the importance of satisfying customers, winning their goodwill, turning them into good ambassadors of the workshop. He led by example.

I wanted to learn woodworking, particularly insofar as it involved the use of the saw, the shaving plane, mallet, hammer, and nails. But my brother would not allow me to meddle with his tools. I felt it unfair that he allowed my younger brother much more freedom with them. It was as if he was actively discouraging my interest in woodworking. If I insisted, he would give me sandpaper to work on some chairs or a table, a very boring, repetitive task. The required standard, it seemed to me, was in the eyes of the judge, and my brother was a very demanding judge. He liked it best when I was holding a book or a newspaper. Then he would draw the attention of his friends to what I was doing.

I did not mind. I had my own agenda. I was waiting for Kenyatta. It was during this period that I got a chance to ride a bike for the first time in my life. Most youth, girls and boys alike, who wanted to learn had to wait for a chance visit by bicycle-owning relatives. As the guests wined and dined, the young would quietly "borrow" the bike and take a ride, as admiring brothers and sisters followed behind, waiting for their turn. Accidents followed, which resulted in beatings when injuries and damage to the bike forced the culprits to confess. But this would not deter them.

I had always wanted to ride a bike but no one I knew had one. And then my half brother Mwangi wa Gacoki, a tailor, rented premises near my brother's furniture shop and opened a grocery store. He shuttled between his tailor and grocery shops, which was hard. At his request, whenever I was not in school I went to the grocery store to help, yet another reason for me to be at the marketplace. Mwangi was married to Elizabeth, sister to Patrick Mũrage Cege, my fellow student at Manguo, with whom I had struck up a friendship.

I don't know how Mũrage got himself a boy's bike, a rare possession, the type we had seen only among Indian youth. He decided to make money by renting it out for a set distance at a time, each ride costing a few cents. I did not have the money needed, so whenever he came to his brother-in-law's shop I would beg him to let me ride his bike for free. But he would not let friendship interfere with commerce. One day I let him have some candy from the shop for free. I did not consider it stealing, as there was so much of it in the big glass container, and, besides, I was not paid for my work, and the shop, I convinced myself, was partly his because it belonged to his brother-in-law. In exchange for the candy, he let me use his bike.

After showing me how to hold the handles and assuring me that pedaling was as easy as drinking a calabash of water, he held the bike as I got on. Then he let it go without telling me he would. Once I started pedaling I panicked. I looked back, and within seconds the bike had veered from the lane outside Mwangi's shop and was going down the slope toward buildings on the opposite side. I did not know how to steer. My legs slipped off the pedals. I was paralyzed with fear. I held on to the handles, my legs spread out in the air. The bike was picking up speed. I was sure I was going to smash into a wall, and then, suddenly, thud! I hit two passersby. They fell, I fell, and the bike lay a few yards away, the wheels spinning. My victims stood up, dusted themselves off, barely avoiding giving me a beating. Fortunately, they were not injured. I did not mind my own bruises for I had escaped a worse fate. Deep inside, though, I thought the fall was punishment for the candy I had stolen.

I did not nurse my wounded pride or body for long; soon something else happened that seized my attention. At a tea shop named the Green Hotel, a few yards away on the same side as the workshop and the grocery store, there was a radio with a loudspeaker, the only one in town. Previously people had relied on readers of Muoria's *Mũmenyereri*, like my friend Ngandi, to relay news to small crowds at a time, who would then spread it even further through word of mouth. Now people crammed inside and outside the tea shop to hear the announcer Mbũrũ Matemo read the news in a voice that would rise and fall. He would shout and whisper for dramatic effect. His listeners increased by the day, as the invisible Mbũrũ Matemo was always prompt at lunchtime when all work in the marketplace would come to a standstill.

It was from the radio that in early October 1952 we heard that Senior Chief Warũhiũ had been assassinated in what Mbũrũ Matemo described as a Chicago gang-style killing, a car trailing the chief's, then pulling alongside, some people dressed in fake police uniforms politely asking the chief to identify himself and then pumping him with bullets before swiftly driving away, and all this in broad daylight. Some days later we heard that Kenyatta had addressed a mammoth rally in Kĩambu, denouncing Mau Mau with the expression: Let it disappear under the roots of the Mikongoe trees *(Mau Mau irothii na miri ya mikongoe)*. Maybe Kenyatta was slowly making his way to Limuru after all. And then on October 20, 1952, came the shocker. Jomo Kenyatta, Bildad Kaggia, Fred Kubai, Paul Ngei, Achieng Oneko, Kũng'ũ Karumba, and other leaders had been arrested, under Operation Jock Scott. Kenyatta had been moved from Gatũndũ to Lokitaung in Turkana, far from Nairobi. Governor Evelyn Baring, who had recently taken over from the previous governor, Philip Mitchell, had declared a state of emergency. Things seemed to be escalating.

Every colonial governor from Eliot in 1902 to Mitchell in 1944 had committed some crime against us, lamented Ngandi, but this was the first time that a governor had declared war on the Kenyan people within a few days of his arrival. Of course, Governor Baring was taking orders from his boss in London, Churchill himself, who was, after all, the prime minister. Do you see the irony? Our own men help him fight Hitler and how does he reward us?

Ngandi had not fought in the Second World War but my half brother Kabae had. I recalled him saying that the world would never know how much African people had contributed to the war effort. I had not seen much of him since leaving my father's house, and I wondered what he would now say about the declaration of war against us, as Ngandi put it. And did the soldiers he came home with that night long ago also feel as Ngandi did about the situation?

Here was another violation of Ngandi's beloved Devonshire declaration. Things would now move from bad to worse to worst before they would start to become better. Ngandi tried to explain the gravity of the situation by decrying the suspension of laws and civil liberties—not that there had been many civil liberties for Africans, but the few that had existed would now be abrogated by martial law. He even talked about other places where a state of emergency had been declared. The British had done it in Ireland in 1939 and in Malaya in 1948. Most ominously, he intoned, Adolf Hitler had done it in Germany in 1933. And what had followed? War. Concentration camps.

As if to confirm Ngandi's suspicions, the radio was soon reporting the landing of British troops, Lancashire Fusiliers, in Nairobi, or, as Ngandi put it, a "convoy" of British military planes had landed at Eastleigh to enhance the existing colonial forces. Some people claimed that they had actually seen the new arrivals patrolling Nairobi streets, armed in very frightening gear. The war machine that had once been directed at Hitler was now turned against us, Ngandi lamented.

The arrest of Jomo Kenyatta may have been a blow to the public, but to me it was personal. It had deprived me of my raison d'être for coming to the marketplace so assiduously. Despite my dashed hopes, the events, even the landing of the British battalions, were largely abstract, happening in a misty land far away, like a story in a distant landscape, alternating between dream and nightmare. Ngandi's citing of emergencies elsewhere and war and concentration camps as well as his scary description of British soldiers and the sweeping arrests in the streets of our capital did not make the story any nearer or more real. Not even when he talked of men entering Nyandarwa and Mount Kenya forests driven by Waiyaki's spirit.

And then things began to hit closer to home. Mau Mau songs and all references to Waiyaki, Kenyatta, or Mbiyũ were criminalized. This abruptly ended my life as a troubadour. More basic, the Kenya Teachers' College at Gĩthũngũri and all KISA and Karĩng'a schools were banned, a blow to my dreams of an education.

I went through a period of uncertainty intensified by conflicting facts and rumors. For some time I stayed away from the Limuru marketplace and the radio at the Green Hotel, getting by on Ngandi's renditions. But I was too used to my brother's workshop and furniture store to keep away from the marketplace for long. Besides, I was now not attending school.

One day I went to the same Limuru marketplace to find men, women, and children bearing luggage, huddled in groups, looking forlorn and lost. The entire marketplace and surrounding areas were occupied by a mass of displaced people. They had been thrown off trains and trucks. This was different from the Ole Ngurueni expulsions of 1948. Those were confined to squatters. Now all Gĩkũyũ, Embu, and Meru people were being expelled from the Rift Valley.

The same scene was taking place at many other centers all over central Kenya. Like the Ole Ngurueni deportees before, most of the new wave had lost all memory of their ancestral origins, for they were descendants of those who had made the Rift Valley their home long ago. This internal displacement continued for weeks.

What I did not know at the time was that my grandmother from Elburgon was herself being displaced.

I grew up envious of children who had grandmothers whom they could visit and who sometimes came to see them with gifts of ripe bananas and sweet potatoes and, most important, the gift of touch and play. Of course I had lots of stepgrandmothers or grandmothers in the Gĩkũyũ extended family system, where every woman of one's grandmother's age group was also one's own. But I could not just go to them, start playing with them, or make demands on them, or expect their embrace and endearments as a natural right. When other kids spoke of their grandmothers, it only accentuated my sense of loss with respect to my paternal grandparents and my absent maternal grandmother. When I had had the chance to take a train to meet her, it had collided with my dreams of school, and I was left with only my younger brother's tales of the glorious time he had spent with Grandmother Gathoni. So although I felt anxious about the cloud from the Rift Valley, I saw and accepted its silver lining: My grandmother had come home.

Whatever had brought about the separation of my two grandparents must still have been fresh, for she stayed in my grandfather's place only briefly after leaving Elburgon.

Then she came to stay with us in our new place, where I got to observe and know her from close quarters.

Her face looked sullen, but when she smiled the folds would go away, and for a time it was nice to cuddle against her. But I had to be careful. Her left arm hung loose, was dead, unfeeling, down to the hand. When seated, she mostly held it in her right hand, stroking its inert fingers. What happened, Grandma?

She never tired of telling the story. She had been all right before and even after relocating to Elburgon to live with her brother Daudi Gatune and her daughter, Auntie Wanjirũ, my mother's only sister, who had by now died, leaving a big daughter, Beatrice, and her young son, named Ngũgĩ like me. And then it happened suddenly. She could not lift her hand. She felt life on her left side leave her; she could actually feel the life draining out of her veins. They took her to the hospital, but the doctors only partially restored some functioning. They could not get to the root of the evil. If she had depended on the hospital alone she would have died. But fortunately a traditional healer was able to penetrate the source of the evil straightaway. A bad person had put several pieces of broken glass inside her body. The healer took them out. I saw them with my own eyes, she would say, almost choking at the memory. A pile of broken pieces of glass. As much as this, she would say, raising her right hand slightly to show the height of the pile. Pieces of a broken bottle, can you imagine that? But Grandmother, shards of glass in your body? Yes, hard, with sharp edges; he took them out in stages. Every time I went back he would discover some more, hidden inside this body. Oh my children, she would tell me, he wanted to kill me, the evil one. If she detected doubts in my reaction, she would become really upset.

Today I assume she must have had a mild stroke, but back then we had no name for it, and we had no facts to contradict her amazing story. Whenever I see pieces of broken glass I always think of my grandmother and her ordeal. For she must have lived with the terror that the evil one would strike again. If she suspected the other woman, or whoever had driven a wedge between her and her husband, as the evil one, she would not say, although she hinted that Mũkami, the youngest wife, had come from Embu or Ndia, places that, from her lips, sounded weirdly far away. Nothing could induce her to take anything, food, water even, from that other woman. She alternated between joy and resentment. When in a joyful mood, she laughed, exposing her still func-tioning full set of white teeth, and she became the grand-mother I had hoped for. But she was mostly resentful, as if everybody had been part of the evil conspiracy and they owed her attention, pity, and service. The more cantanker-ous she became, the more the glamour of having a grand-mother wore off.

She had this incredible hold on my mother. There was nothing that my mother could do that seemed to mollify my grandmother and put her in good humor, which forced my mother to intensify her efforts to care for her, to meet her demands, spoken and often unspoken. My grandmother would be talking to us in a friendly almost relaxed manner, but the moment her own daughter approached, she would instinctively revert to her injured self, sighing and hinting neglect or loudly blaming her own body for preventing her from doing things for herself. Tension mounted in the house.

To reduce the contention between mother and grandmother, Good Wallace put up another hut for my grandmother on a separate site, next to my mother's, hoping that this would give her more independence and my mother some peace. But even in her new abode, my grandmother expected instant service from her daughter. The situation became worse, my grandmother now openly and continuously complaining of neglect. The only other name whose mention made her even more resentful and made her complain even more, was my grandfather's. But they did not see much of each other, and when they did sarcastic barbs would fly from my grandmother's mouth and her husband would walk away.

And then a shadow of death fell on my grandfather's house.

Kĩmũchũ's house was literally on the other side of my grandfather's compound. He was in the process of putting the finishing touches on a new stone house next to the old one of wood slabs with its corrugated iron roof. A white man, a British officer, with a gang of African paramilitary, came for Kĩmũchũ by night. His wife assumed that he had been arrested the way Kenyatta and others had been. But when she and other relatives inquired at police stations they got no news. After a few days what had happened became clear. Kĩmũchũ, Njerandi, Elijah Karanja, Mwangi,

Nehemiah, some of the most prominent men in Limuru, all picked up the same night, had been summarily executed by the British officer at a wooded glen in Kĩneniĩ, a few yards from the road built by the Bonos. Ndũng'ũ and Njoroge, Kĩmũchũ's children by his first wife, Wangũi, had now lost both parents.

Terror struck our region, but it hit my grandfather hardest. He was Kĩmũchũ's surrogate father; they were very close. My grandfather was convinced he would be next, that "they" would come for him by night. He sought refuge in my mother's hut. Every evening, under the cover of darkness, he would slip into our place. To see this very powerful man, the respected landowner and custodian of his subclan, yes, my grandfather who wrote letters to the government, in our hut, quaking with fear of colonial malfeasance, was my first real intimation of the import of the state of emergency. He had to use a chamber pot. I felt with him his painful humiliation at having to use a chamber pot in his own daughter's hut! After a few weeks he relaxed and returned to his normal residence with Mũkami. But now and then he would still seek out our place at night.

For the duration of his struggle, my grandmother became less sullen, more sympathetic. An undeclared truce reigned between them. But after he left and the white shadow of death did not strike again, life returned to normal in my mother's house, which also meant the return of Grandmother's sullenness, and my mother's terror of her own mother. My grandmother complained of her displacement from Elburgon before the healer had completed his task. The pieces of broken glass that the healer had not taken out still hurt.

Then came the week when my grandmother turned kind and gentle. She was loving and comforting, and I wished she would always be like that. She joked a little, and laughed softly. People could talk about anything without her bringing up the pieces of glass that unknown evil had planted in her.

Kĩmũchũ's brutal assassination was always alluded to in a variety of ways: What was going to happen to all his wealth? Would Phyllis, his widow, look after the property in the equal interests of all the children, hers and her stepchildren? This would lead to discussions about Ndũng'ũ, Kĩmũchũ's eldest son, who was about my age, and Njoroge, his younger brother. Ndũng'ũ was going to be a man soon, my mother said, reporting what she heard as coming from Ndũng'ũ's grandmother. Then he would look after the portion of wealth due to him.

My grandmother turned to me: "And my husband here? He cannot be left behind." She called me her husband because I was named after my grandfather. I laughed off the talk of becoming a man. I was focused on school only. The idea of circumcision was very far from my mind. But for some reason she would not let the matter go, and a few days later she brought up the subject, reiterating that Ndũng'ũ, who was my age, could not become a man and leave me behind a boy. I tried to distract her by asking her more details about the story of the removal of the pieces of glass from her body. Previously this would have been sure bait. I was surprised by her mild response.

"I have no ill will toward the evil one," she said, and then continued in the same train of thought. "I have never meant anybody harm."

It was as if, by asking questions about her condition, I had induced in her forgiveness and general beneficence. She kept on telling my mother and all of us that she harbored no bad feelings toward anybody. As if to confirm the truth of it, she slightly spit on her hands and breast in the Gĩkũyũ gesture of blessing.

She went to bed. She never woke up again. She had peacefully passed to the next world. My mother's tears expressed deep sadness and relief. In the evening after the burial we sat around the fireside, with shadows and light playing on our faces.

"Your grandmother was a good woman; it was the illness that had turned her against joy," my mother said as if to fill the emptiness we all felt. I really missed her. I missed the grandmother I had and the one I could have had.

"She did not harbor any bad feelings toward this or any other house," my mother continued slowly as if partly to reassure herself.

It was then that I realized my mother had all along been scared that, in her bitterness against life, my grandmother might leave a curse behind. A parent's curse, even if not directly voiced, could take effect as a result of any bad words they may have spoken in their last days on earth. A curse could also follow failure to meet their wishes expressed before their passing on. A last wish is a final command.

"She said that Ndũng'ũ cannot leave you behind," my mother said, turning toward me, in a manner that brooked no demur.

The ban on Karĩng'a and KISA schools, especially the Kenya Teachers' College at Gĩthũngũri, was a practical and psychological assault on the African initiative for self-reliance. Much had gone into their organization. Mbiyũ Koinange had narrowly escaped arrest alongside Kenyatta because he happened to be in England at the time, representing the Kenya African Union. Many others associated with the college were among the thousands arrested. But the biggest blow to the collective psyche occurred when the colonial state turned the college grounds and buildings into a prison camp where proponents of resistance to colonialism were hanged.

Ngandi almost wept at the news. His beloved alma mater turned into a slaughterhouse for nationalists? But the eternal optimist in him would reappear and he would assert that Mbiyũ had not been spared by God for nothing. He would come back. Remember? From America, he brought back Hampton and Tuskegee combined; from England he will bring us Oxford and Cambridge. One way or another Gĩthũngũri would be restored.

The fact that Manguo, a Karĩng'a school, would be no

more affected me directly and immediately. Up to then there had been two competing and parallel systems of modern education, that of the government and the missionaries on one hand, and the African-run independent schools on the other. I had been able to move from one to the other. And now? There was no choice. I was not even sure that Kamandūra would take me back.

I don't know how long I lived with the uncertainty. But the following year, 1953, it was announced that a number of KISA and Karĩng'a schools would be reopened under government control. Some trustees refused to give up their independence and hence their schools did not reopen. Many others were not given that option. Manguo was among those whose board members agreed to have the school reopened under the government-sanctioned Kĩambu District Education Board. The syllabus would be determined by colonial masters.

The effects were immediate. In the new Manguo, music and performance died. The interschool sports festival became a thing of memory. The marching band too. The school was no longer the center of local communal festivities. Some of the old teachers including Fred Mbũgua lost their jobs. Stephen Thiro was retained as acting headmaster pending the arrival of a newly appointed one from Kagumo, a government-approved training college.

There was a subtle shift in emphasis in the teaching of certain subjects like history and English. In the old school, teachers told us about African kings like Shaka, Cetshwayo. They told us a bit about the white conquest and settlements in South Africa and Kenya. But now the emphasis was on white explorers like Livingstone, Stanley, Rebman, and Krapf. We learned in positive terms about the establishment of Christian missions. We learned that white people had discovered Mount Kenya and many of our lakes, including Lake Victoria. In the old school, Kenya was a black man's country. In the new school, Kenya, like South Africa, was represented as having been sparsely populated before the whites arrived, and so whites occupied the uninhabited areas. Where, as in Tigoni in Limuru, they had taken African lands, the previous occupants had been compensated. There had also been tribal wars. White people brought medicine, progress, peace. The teachers were of course following the official government-approved syllabus under which students would eventually be examined.

A European inspector of schools, a Mr. Doran or some such name, started making the rounds to ensure compliance. His visits were often unannounced, and once on the grounds he expected teachers to run to him and stand at attention the whole time he talked to them. Sometimes he would park his car some distance away and surreptitiously approach the grounds. He would enter a classroom, stand at the back, watch as the teacher conducted class, and then walk to the blackboard, take chalk, and strike out any word that was spelled wrong or any sentence with incorrect grammar and then write the correct words and sentence on top. There was general unease as the teachers tried to make light of it or even pretend gratitude. At first we were half delighted to see somebody else doing to the teacher what the teachers did to us, but as it became a habit we started sharing the teachers' humiliation. We may have laughed about it, and even talked about it among ourselves, but it was really to hide our embarrassment.

We did not know how strongly we felt about this until Josephat Karanja, a student from Makerere University College, Uganda, came to teach in the school during his long vacation. Karanja was from Gĩthũngũri, the neighboring region. He was always meticulously dressed in gray trousers, a cardigan over a white shirt, and a tie, his hair parted on the side. At first we were excited to have a Makerere student for a teacher, but we soon wished we could do without his services. He used the stick too frequently against students who made mistakes persistently and even against those who did so occasionally.

One day the white inspector drove to the school and stood outside on the grounds leaning against his car as he frequently did. The other teachers ran to him, but Karanja did not. The inspector must have sent one of the other teachers to ask Karanja to come to him. We sensed a drama in the making, and as Karanja left the room we stood on our desks and peered through the windows. The inspector was hopping mad, beckoning Karanja to run. We hoped that Karanja would be disciplined before all our eyes. But Karanja did not change his pace. Even when the inspector shouted, Hurry up, Karanja refused to alter his pace. Now they stood face-to-face. The inspector wanted Karanja to call him sir, but Karanja just looked at him and then walked back to class. Aware that many eyes were watching, the officer hung around for a minute or so and then he got into his car and drove away. We never saw him again.

We retook our seats, but as Karanja entered we all stood up in deference, not fear. He was a hero. He had restored something we had lost, pride in our teachers, pride in ourselves. We hoped that he would come back again. But he did not. He was expelled from Makerere for leading or taking part in a student strike. He completed his undergraduate degree in India and then went on to Princeton, in the United States, later achieving success as independent Kenya's first high commissioner in London. Eventually he returned to the country and became a disastrous vice-chancellor of the University of Nairobi under Kenyatta and a short-lived vice president for Dictator Moi. Somehow I always recall that moment in a primary school in colonial Kenya when he refused to accede to humiliation.

An African inspector would come next, James Mũigai, actually Kenyatta's stepbrother, who was much friendlier. Sporting a helmet and goggles, he was impressive on his motorbike and used to brag about his bike being a BMC, Birmingham Motor Corporation, product. No matter how many times he visited, he never forgot to say that he was riding a BMC. I don't think he was consciously hiding the fact, but he never mentioned his relationship to Kenyatta or talked about what was happening in the land.

Although the study of religion had not been a requirement at the old Manguo school, and I was not a convert to the orthodox or any Christian faith, I missed Kĩhang'ũ's Sunday performances, which had come to an end with the banning of the African Orthodox Church. Now there was no church associated with the government school. But other churches did try to provide a home for these lost souls.

Indeed, some of those who had been followers of the orthodox faith did try other churches. But for the many faithful, going back to a church associated with missionaries, like Kamandũra, was anathema. For others the Catholic Church seemed the rightful place. It had not been hostile to orthodox followers. It did not confront those who practiced polygamy or wanted to marry their traditions with Christian faith. Indeed, the Catholic Church as a whole had refused to take a hard line in the female circumcision conflict of the 1920s. It was less judgmental in its criteria for admission into its fold. The church at Limuru Loreto Convent was one of the oldest Christian institutions in the area. Many students at Manguo started drifting there, as word spread that admission was easy. You reported there and you came back a

Catholic! Later we were shocked when Stephen Thiro's sister, Hegara Gacambi, the daughter of Kĩeya, the founding patriarch of Manguo Karĩng'a, was granted a place in high school and chose to become a nun.

Kenneth Mbũgua and I too decided to become Catholics. My friendship with Kenneth, whose father was Fred Mbũgua, who years earlier had read aloud my Gĩkũyũ essay, had started off on the wrong foot in the days when I still lived in my father's house. The route from my father's house to the Indian shops passed near Kenneth's home. Kenneth was big for his age and was a bully. He used to terrify my younger brother and me, sometimes threatening to confiscate our tire rims that we drove with sticks as our "cars." When I told my mother about the threat, she spoke to his mother, Josephine, but Kenneth did not stop harassing us: Things got even worse. My mother hated conflicts, and she would have been the first to scold me if she knew that I had caused a fight. I reported Kenneth to my mother again. She said, Do you want me to fight him for you? I realized that there would be no more help from that quarter, but at the same time I realized that she would not scold me for defending myself.

One day Kenneth threatened us again and expected us to take to our heels, but this time I stood my ground and dared him to touch me. He stepped toward me, and angry and furious I lurched at him. Taken by surprise, he fell to the ground and I was on him. Quickly recovering from the shock, he struggled to get the upper hand by turning me over. I had not the slightest doubt that he had the strength to overpower me but I was determined not to let him. My younger brother, who had fled, now came back, and together we pinned him to the ground. We gave him a few blows, and then we ran away as he chased us swearing revenge but with less and less conviction in his voice. He never did avenge our presumed impertinence. Instead we gradually became friends, especially after I moved from Kamandũra to Manguo school and my father's house, because our new home was a couple of fields from Kenneth's. That was my first lesson in the virtue of resistance, that right and justice can empower the weak.

In the classroom at school Kenneth and I were emerging as academic rivals, but the gap between us two and the rest of the class was huge and this enhanced our friendship. I don't know what made Kenneth and me decide to become Catholics. His father in those days was rather indifferent to church matters. His mother was very religious and she always went to Kamandũra church even when her husband had been the academic pillar of Manguo in its Karĩng'a stage. Kenneth had been baptized as a child and I had not. I don't remember that we talked about Catholicism deeply. It is quite possible that we were merely following a fad. Without telling or consulting anybody, we set a date when we would walk to Limuru Loreto Convent and come back as Roman Catholics.

It was one of those coincidences difficult to explain. On the way, near the Limuru African marketplace, we met his mother. When Josephine learned where we were going and the reason, she was horrified. There was no way we were going to be Catholics, she said firmly. If it was baptism I wanted, and reaffirmation in the case of Kenneth, she would take us to Lord Reverend Stanley Kahahu for registration in his baptismal classes.

I am still conflicted in my relationship to the Kahahus. We had left their domain but we still go there for work. Once Lillian Kahahu, saying that she was helping us, gives me and my younger brother an acre to weed. The money she offers sounds huge in the light of our needs. Lillian looks even more generous when she gives us half the amount as down payment, the rest to be paid after we complete the task. It takes us months to make a dent, and by then the money is not anywhere near worth the labor we have put into the job. We are in a bind; we can't stop working because we cannot pay back what we have already received. My mother hates debt, and we still need the tiny income. I will not work there again, I tell myself when we finally complete the task.

In no time need once again compels me to join the seasonal labor force to pick pyrethrum flowers. We are many, adults and children, from different corners of the village. Some kids, hungry and thirsty, jump over the fence into the Kahahus' orchard and pick some plums. I am not one of them. My mother would kill me for stealing, and her definition of theft is very wide. Lillian discovers the theft and in the evening, when we take our pick for weighing, she asks the culprits to give themselves up or for the innocents to tell on them. It is Friday evening. Our wages for the week are due. She repeats her demand. The guilty do not give themselves up; the innocent do not tell on them. Then comes the judgment. We are all going to lose our wages unless we hand over the culprits.

I cannot believe my ears. Does she know how desperately we need this money at home? No, she cannot be serious. But she is. No one, not even the adults among us, protests. The unfairness of it all cuts deeply into me. I step forward. I raise my voice. All eyes turn to me! You cannot do this: It is not right, I find myself telling her. She recovers from the shock. Yes, I shall, unless the culprits give themselves up, she says coolly. And you call yourself a Christian? I ask. All mouths fall open. Lillian, the wife of Lord Reverend Stanley Kahahu, the manager of the estate, has never been challenged by any of her workers. She hires and fires at will. But I know that everyone present knows that I am right. Still no other voice joins in expressing discontent. Your Christianity is without meaning, I say and leave the scene, tears of anger and frustration streaming down my face.

This episode becomes the talk of the village. Ngũgĩ, Wanjikũ's quiet son known for his polite demeanor and deference to age, has said words that no child should speak to an adult, some would say. But others would say that Lillian had gone too far—punishing the guilty and the innocent for a few plums? And pocketing a whole week of wages as vengeance? Parents protest. Lillian gives in, but pays reduced wages. She does not pay me. My loss is the gain of others. Here was my second lesson in resistance. She goes to see my mother to protest. My mother does not respond. I know she does not condone a younger person's rudeness to an adult. She does not scold me. I am not working for the Kahahus anymore, I tell my mother, and she agrees. I had lost my hard-won wages but I felt free.

These thoughts are swirling in my head after Kenneth's mother tells me she is going to take us by the hand to Reverend Kahahu. Despite Lillian's unfairness, I still appreciate Reverend Kahahu's role in the recovery of my eyesight. I make a distinction between the Reverend Kahahu, the preacher, and his wife, Lillian, the manager. Besides, Kenneth's mother is not taking us to his house, only to the church.

I yielded and registered with Reverend Kahahu for baptism. Thus began my religious classes at Kamandũra. There was the catechism to memorize, then a test, and after passing it one had to choose Christian names. I was weighing James Paul. Both were the baptismal names of Kahahu's children. Reverend Kahahu said one name was sufficient. And so, by the Christian rite of baptism by water, I became James Ngũgĩ, the name under which years later I would publish my early journalism and fiction until 1969, when I reverted to Ngũgĩ wa Thiong'o.

I have always been conscious of the irony of my situation. After narrowly escaping becoming a Roman Catholic, I had joined a Church of Scotland Mission congregation while attending a government school, formerly a Karĩng'a that had been linked to the African Orthodox Church, now also banned. By this time the CSM had changed its name to the Presbyterian Church of East Africa.

I extended the irony: On Sundays I went to Kamandũra for worship and spiritual communion; on weekdays to Manguo for a life of the mind.

In the new Manguo school, English was still emphasized as the key to modernity, but, whereas in the Karĩng'a Manguo, English and Gĩkũyũ coexisted, now Gĩkũyũ was frowned upon. The witch hunt for those speaking African languages in the school compound began, the consequence rising to bodily punishment in some cases. A teacher would give a piece of metal to the first student he caught speaking an African language. The culprit would pass it to the next person who repeated the infraction. This would go on the whole day, and whoever was the last to have the metal in his possession would be beaten. Sometimes the metal was inscribed with demeaning words or phrases like "Call me stupid." I saw teachers draw blood from students. Despite this we were proud of our English proficiency and eager to practice the new language outside the school compound.

An opportunity came, unexpectedly. As part of its efforts to win minds and hearts, the Department of Information had started a magazine, *Pamoja*, to teach civics and spread good words about government services. Kenneth was the first among us to write a letter to the Department of Information, Nairobi, to ask for the magazine. He got a formal reply in an envelope with an official-looking stamp on it. It was a few lines only, thanking him for his inquiry and telling him that they would be sending him a copy. It was amazing. He had written a letter in English by hand and got a typed reply that actually thanked him? And also signed "your faithful servant"? A couple of days later he received the magazine. I asked Kenneth to show me how he had done it, the letter he had written, the address, everything. I wrote a similar letter, almost word for word, sent it under my name, and got the same reply addressing me as "Dear Sir" and signed "your faithful servant." Soon I too was the proud recipient of the magazine, on which was typed: James Ngugi, c/o Manguo School, PO Box 66, Limuru.

Though identical to what Kenneth and other students had received, the reply and my name on the magazine thrilled me. I kept on gazing at it. I took it home to my mother, proudly announcing that the government had written me a letter. Previously, my grandfather had been the only family member I had seen with letters from the government. And why would the government be writing to you? she asked rather suspiciously. I explained that I had initiated the correspondence. In English, I added, to impress her.

The wonder of "my" English words eliciting a written response took me back to the times when my younger brother and I used to try out our knowledge of a few words of another language on native speakers. It was at my father's house. When she had a good harvest or whenever her granary had corn, potatoes, beans, or peas, my mother was generous with food. She always cooked enough to feed those present as well as unexpected guests. I remember times when itinerant Kamba women traders, complete strangers, would stop by and she would let them stay the night and feed them to the best of her ability. My older brothers and sisters never announced who they would bring home. If a visitor came and left without being treated to a cup of porridge at least, my mother felt bad, as if she had failed in some way. Some of the more regular callers, visiting with Good Wallace mostly, were workers at the Limuru Bata Shoe factory. They were from different Kenyan communities and from them we learned a few simple words and phrases, for greetings mostly. From Luo, we learned to ask: *Idhi nade?* From Kamba: *Nata? Wĩ mũseo?* From Luhya, *Mrembe?* But how could we be sure that we really knew the words? Or that, from our own lips, they could elicit a response from a native speaker other than those who had taught us the phrases?

One of my mother's parcels of land was near the road that led from the Bata shoe workers' resident camp, through the African marketplace, opposite Karabu's place, to the Indian shops. We used to work that parcel, helping my mother with weeding and mulching. There was always human traffic between the Indian shopping center and the African shops. We decided that it was time to test our knowledge of the languages we had learned. But we had trouble in telling who was Kamba, Luhya, or Luo among the passersby. Waiting near the road and hidden by the cornstalks, we watched and listened for non-Gĩkũyũ speakers. We were lucky with our first attempt. We guessed correctly that they were a group of Luo workers. We suddenly emerged from the cornfield. *Idhi nade?* The startled group answered something like: *Adhi ma ber.* We did not have enough words to continue. *Ero kamano,* I said, and my brother, *Ahero,* as we dashed back into the cornfields, excited that we had been understood, but not wanting our knowledge to be tested further. We did the same for Kikamba and Kiluhya. Sometimes we failed to connect, but whenever we did we felt the same excitement as we went back to the cover of the cornstalks.

That was oral communication. Now I was writing English and undergoing a similar sensation, knowing that I had been understood by an unknown reader who had written a response to my English words even though I had copied them from Kenneth. Years later I would feel a similar thrill at the acceptance of my first pieces of writing in a school magazine or at a publisher's positive response to my book manuscript.

There were unforeseen consequences to that letter signed by "your faithful servant." Having given my name and address, I would continue to get not only the particular information bulletin but several other government publications, in English. Without the *Mũmenyereri* and other African-language publications, the only alternative to government radio and English-language newspaper was oral media.

The oral news in Gĩkũyũ and the accounts written in English often gave conflicting views of the same events, which I found confusing at times. At first the contradiction did not matter. Being able to read an English publication was more important than the information gleaned. The medium trumped the message. Then one day I received a broadsheet titled "Lari Massacre," and I could no longer ignore the message.

The Lari region neighbored Limuru, about twelve miles away. In March 1953 the colonial chief of Lari, Luka wa Kahangara, and some of his family were killed. The publication carried gruesome pictures of human bodies and carcasses of cows rotting in the open fields. It also carried pictures of Governor Baring and the British colonial secretary, Oliver Lyttelton, visiting the scene. The pictures spoke louder than the words accompanying them: They disturbed me extremely, more so because of the seeming senselessness. The images, arranged as they were, suggested irrational behavior, acts without rhyme or reason.

I showed the publication to Mzee Ngandi when later he came to visit with my elder brother. This is bad, very bad, I said. He looked at it, read a little bit. He was his usual pensive self. But this time he did not whistle to himself as he often did. He took out a copy of the *East African Standard*. With the banning of *Mũmenyereri*, the English-language *East African Standard* had taken its place in the outer pockets of his jacket. He said, You find the same in this settler newspaper, the headlines, the pictures, the story. Every event has more than one side to it. What you are seeing and reading is the colonial view. The freedom fighters have no newspaper or radio in which to voice their own side. So don't believe everything that you read in these documents. It is propaganda.

That word was a new one to me. But look at these, I said,

pointing at the pictures of the dead, as if to say there were no two sides to what I saw before me.

By this time there was a group of listeners around him, the kind of atmosphere in which he thrived. It was true that there had been killings at Lari. But remember this: The guerrillas are under strict orders from Marshall Dedan Kĩmathi not to kill at random. The guerrillas could not survive without support from the people. So why would they kill indiscriminately? The roots of the tragedy, he explained, went back to the European occupation of our land, which they then baptized White Highlands. But look for Lari in the First World War. I recalled the story of how my father had avoided the war. What had the Lari killings in 1953 to do with the English and the Germans fighting in 1914–1918?

You see (he said), after the First World War, what remained of the African-owned lands in Tigoni, or Kanyawa, were taken over to settle more English people, under the soldier settlement scheme. Do you see the unfairness? English soldiers go to war and are rewarded with land taken from Africans. Africans go to the same war as fighters and Carrier Corps and are rewarded with having their lands stolen. It was the same with the Second World War. Jobs for the returning European soldier; joblessness for the African fighter. Now about Kanyawa. The African families affected refused alternative settlements. You see, after the 1923 Devonshire declaration, Kenya was a black man's country; in a conflict between Africans and other races over land, African rights were paramount. The families knew that the rights of inheritance, law, and justice were on their side.

They swore to stand together or fall together. In 1927 Luka Kahangara, a spokesperson, broke ranks. He agreed to move to alternative lands in Lari. He gave the British legal cover for the theft. Those who held out were moved by force, their houses torched. They lost their land and houses. Some moved to Ndeiya and other places. The Lari killings, even though they look bad, are not crazy acts. Chief Luka's house and the houses of his followers were torched in the same way that the houses of the rightful Tigoni dwellers had been torched by the colonial police. I don't like tooth-for-tooth justice. But look at it this way: While the Mau Mau fighters targeted the chief, his family, and their followers, the colonial forces acted as if every other person alive must be guilty of the killings. They executed people, their bodies left out in the open or in the forests to rot.

Ngandi told the story of a man from Lari, one of several who were tied together with a rope and made to stand in a line. A British officer asked his African askaris to open fire. When they hesitated, he opened fire himself, with a machine gun. The captives fell in a heap. To make sure that they were all dead, the officer shot another round of machine-gun fire on those who had already fallen. He and his men went away. But one man, he did not die. Not a bullet touched him. When in the morning villagers came to look at the bodies, the man raised his head. At first they retreated a distance, thinking that he was a ghost. But they hearkened to his feeble cry for help. The man comes to Limuru market shops. I will point him out to you, he assured me and continued. Unfortunately, he has lost his power of speech, Ngandi added. He was the lucky one. There were hundreds of others who did not survive, butchered by the colonial forces that night and the following days. Then they blame all the killings on the Mau Mau guerrillas. Why? They want the fighters to look bad. They also want the eyes of the world to look away from what really fueled their anger. On the night of the attacks on Luka's compound at Lari, the Naivasha police station also fell to the freedom fighters. The guerrillas released the prisoners, broke open the armory, and took away many guns and ammunition. Do you find the story in the press? Do you find it in the publication they send to you? You remember Mbũrũ Matemo the radio announcer? You will never hear his voice again. He has been dismissed because he mentioned that Naivasha had fallen to the guerrilla fighters. Now he is in a concentration camp like thousands of others. The Lari massacre is a massacre, all right, but it is also a British massacre in retaliation for the death of a loyal chief and the fall of the Naivasha police station, Ngandi asserted conclusively.

The Lari killings and the fall of the Naivasha police station were followed by other government actions that brought the effects of the state of emergency to ordinary lives outside the main cities. The colonial state had already formed a new force drawn from loyalist elements in the population called Home Guards. Now more and more were recruited into the force. Increasingly this force became one of the most brutal instruments of colonial terror. Their local center of visible power in our area was a Home Guard post built atop the highest ridge at Kamĩrĩthũ. The most prominent feature of the post, really a fort, was a tall watchtower, guarded day and night by armed gunmen. Surrounding the fort was a dry moat into which wooden spikes were planted so that if anyone fell on them, he would be pierced fatally. The moat was reinforced by thick barbed wire. The only way in and out of the fort was via a drawbridge, which was raised at night and lowered in the daytime. Home Guards slept inside the camp. Functioning as a military command center, a police precinct, and a prison, the Home Guard post was a chamber of horrors.

Older chiefs like Njiriri wa Mũkoma and local headmen like his brother Kĩmunya, deemed to be friendly to the people, were replaced by others more fiercely loyal to the colonial state and aggressively hostile to nationalist fighters and the population. One of the most notorious was headman Ragae, who outdid others in cruelty, particularly against those who had been internally displaced from the Rift Valley. What was it that could make a person turn so brutal toward his own people? I used to wonder about this man who always walked with a rifle slung on his shoulder and with an armed bodyguard. One day some guerrillas stalked him as he ambled from Limuru marketplace to the Home Guard post and shot him, on the roadside. They left him for dead, but he survived. Later, disguised as doctors, they entered the hospital where he had been admitted and finished him off. Ragae was not mourned by anybody. Instead, people rejoiced openly.

One of the tasks of the chief, the village headman, and the Home Guards was enforcing communal labor assignments and compulsory attendance at *barazas*, government meetings on certain days of the week. During a chief's *baraza* and communal labor—cutting grass, digging terraces, sweeping streets, anything that met the whims of the chief—all shops had to close. No one was allowed to work on their parcels of land. Even schoolkids were sometimes swept into the meetings. Those who were absent from communal labor and government meetings were arrested and held in the Home Guard post for days. Both of these forced exercises seriously disrupted production and contributed to mass hunger and weakening of the population.

I was once forced to attend the chief's *barazas*, where he spent the time preaching the virtues of obedience to the state and taunting his listeners with "your Kenyatta will not walk from the Kapenguria Court, free. He will hang at Gĩthũngũri."

For me the trial of Jomo Kenyatta becomes a vast oral performance narrated and directed by Mzee Ngandi with the ease and authority of an eyewitness. I presume that Ngandi, like some of his audience, has to read between the lines of the settler-owned newspapers and government radio. But he enriches what he gleans here and there with rich creative interpretation. His narration is influenced by his conviction that Kenyatta will win. This more than anything else helps his listeners to willingly suspend all disbelief.

Ngandi has never been to Kapenguria, or any part of Turkana, but he begins by setting the scene: a couple of shops, a narrow dusty road, a dilapidated schoolhouse turned into a courtroom in a vast arid land of stunted grass, cactus, a thorn tree here and there, and herdsmen, with their goats and cows, who suddenly look up to see cars, armed police, white people they had not seen before, come and go, every day for weeks and months.

He introduces the cast of international and local players. Heading the cast is one who is actually absent from Judge Ransley Thacker's court: Mbiyũ Koinange, KAU delegate, free in England, turns out to be the genius behind the formidable cast of defense lawyers, aided, no doubt, by his old friends, Fenner Brockway and others of the Labor Party. What do you expect? Ngandi asks his audience rhetorically. The mind that once organized Kenya Teachers' College at Gĩthũngũri, bringing different people together in a common pursuit, is at it again.

Then follows D. N. Pritt, the lead defense attorney, no ordinary lawyer; he is a QC, Queen's Counsel, which means that he advises the head of the British Empire, Ngandi explains, strongly hinting that the queen may not have been very pleased with Governor Baring's hasty act of arresting Kenyatta. Kenya is her favorite country, he asserts, quickly reminding his audience that she was transformed from princess to queen while honeymooning at the Treetops lodge, near Nyeri. See? On February 6, 1952, she learns she has become a queen while on Kenyan soil; in October 1952 she hears that her prime minister, Churchill, and her representative here, Governor Baring, have had Kenyatta arrested.

Other members of the defense team have come from all parts of the queen's empire, including Dudley Thompson from Jamaica and H. O. Davies from Nigeria. Others from all corners of the world have been denied entry at the airport in their attempt to work with the three local lawyers, Fitz de Souza, Jaswant Singh, and A. Kapila. Kapila is second to D. N. Pritt in brilliance. If Kapila lived in England, he would have long ago joined the secret group of Queen's Counsels. Jawaharlal Nehru himself, the prime minister of India, has sent lawyer Chaman Lall, a member of Parliament, to join the team.

The fact that the prime minister of India has sent lawyers is a very significant contribution to Ngandi's certainty of victory. The British had colonized India for hundreds of years. Led by Mahatma Gandhi and Nehru, Indian people demanded their independence. Just like our people are now doing, led by Jomo Kenyatta and Mbiyũ Koinange. And look at their leader. He describes the frail figure of Mahatma Gandhi, dressed in a loincloth they call a dhoti, and how Indians all over the world loved him and hang his picture on the walls of their shops. Mahatma Gandhi? Their leader? A loincloth? That was the very picture I used to see hanging on the walls of the Limuru Indian shops. I had taken it that he was one of the Indian gods because my mother had once told me so.

They got theirs in 1947, Ngandi continues with his infectious logic of optimism. There is no reason we should not get ours in 1957. Gandhi fought the British with truth; Kenyatta will smite the British Empire with his call for justice. India led the way.

Ngandi tells the story of India's long relationship to Kenya, which starts long before the railway and the string of railroad towns. Before Europeans came to East Africa, there were Indian traders in Mombasa and Malindi already. The pilot who showed that rascal Vasco da Gama the route to India across the ocean was an Indian resident at the coast.

Against demurring voices, for his listeners have not seen any Limuru Indian involved in public affairs or being forced to attend the chief's *barazas* and participate in communal labor, he uses the occasion to talk positively about the Indian contribution to the Kenyan struggle. Strange that his listeners could earlier have accepted with delight the story of Makhan Singh as a prophet and yet be skeptical about the Indian role now. But Ngandi soldiers on and cites cases of Indian organizations and individuals working with Africans at different stages of the Kenyan struggle, including giving office space and printing facilities to African-language newspapers and magazines. He mentions the Desai alliance with Harry Thuku in the 1920s and Gandhi's expression of solidarity with the imprisoned Thuku.

Ngandi may or may not have known that documentary evidence was on his side. But when the workers' leader was arrested and detained in Kismayu, then part of Kenya, Gandhi himself wrote in the paper *Young India* that Thuku was the victim of "lust for power," and that if Thuku "ever saw these lines, he will perhaps find comfort in the thought that even in distant India many will read the story of his deportation and trials with sympathy."*

Every workers' strike from Harry Thuku's times to the 1947 strikes that spread to Uplands Bacon factory and Limuru Bata Shoe Company had had Indian support, Ngandi asserts.

I had personal knowledge of some of the strikers. One of the Bata workers, Kĩariĩ, who used to come to my mother's house, ended up marrying my eldest sister, Gathoni, and took her to his place in Kĩambaa near Koinange's. After he lost his job, he went back to Kĩambaa to farm and complain

---

* *Young India*, December 18, 1924. Reprinted in *Collected Works of Mahatma Gandhi* vol. 25, p. 398, http://www.anc.org.za/ancdocs/history/people/gandhi/anil.html.

about the Bata Boers. Every white man was a Boer to my brother-in-law.

Indians are not all from Limuru, Ngandi would say, citing others like Gama Pinto, ending with the case of Ida Dass, who accompanied Mbiyũ to England. And now you see the good work that Mbiyũ is doing rallying support abroad for this trial.

From Ngandi's lips, the trial of Jomo Kenyatta becomes geography, history, politics, civics, and above all myth. In his retelling, the places mentioned in the trial—Manchester, Moscow, Denmark—become backdrops in a huge fictional territory in which Ngandi engages the inhabitants, sometimes in embrace, sometimes in fury. He is a narrator who takes sides in the struggle between his characters. He has nothing but contempt for Thacker, an old settler, retrieved from the dump yard of retirement to sit, on behalf of the settler community, in judgment of a nationalist. Having already made up his mind, Thacker does not even pretend to listen to evidence: Instead he plays with his glasses, nods off, occasionally waking up to say no to motions by the defense and yes to those by the prosecution. Ngandi argues with Anthony Somerhough, the prosecutor, and his witnesses, some of whom, like Louis Leakey, the court interpreter, arouse in him genuine anger. Louis Leakey grew up among us, the son of Canon Leakey; he even befriended the Koinange family. Mbiyũ was the best man at his wedding with Mary. He is a spy. He learned Gĩkũyũ so that he could report about us from the inside. That is why he is called Karwĩgĩ, "Hawk." He is actually a Trojan horse.

I know next to nothing about horses, least of all the Trojan type, and Ngandi takes the time to explain. I am one of his most attentive listeners, and he is more expansive when I am in the crowd. In my presence he injects more English phrases and sentences, and my seeming to understand what he says serves as confirmation of his knowledge to the others.

His real ire is mostly directed at the African prosecution witnesses like Rawson Macaria and Gĩciriri. Traitors, he would say, annoyed that he and some of these witnesses breathe the same Limuru air, although now and then he tempers his anger by saying, Lord forgive them for they know not what they are doing.

The mention of Gĩciriri interferes with the mythical plane in which the characters have been moving. I have seen him in Limuru. Everybody knows him; he's a friend of the assassinated Kĩmũchũ even. One of his children, Wanjikũ, has been in the same school with me. Very nice, very agreeable, and she does not seem like the daughter of the ogre emerging from Ngandi's narrative. Still, every time I think of Gĩciriri, I shiver a little: I cannot see how any African would ever agree to testify against his own people, especially in this case, since one of the Kapenguria Six, Kũng'ũ Karumba, comes from Ndeiya in Limuru.

Ngandi's representation of things seen and yet unseen in different locales, repeated over many days, helps replace the gloom of despair with a glow of hope. Looked at from every conceivable angle, the case for Kenyatta's release will prevail. In time I come to share the same certainty: Kenyatta and the rest of the Kapenguria Six, as the defendants have been dubbed, shall win.

So when on April 8, 1953, it emerges that Kenyatta and the others have been found guilty and sentenced to seven years of hard labor, my heart falls. What went wrong? How could the queen, Nehru, and all those lawyers from all the corners of the empire allow this? Bewildered, I turn to Ngandi, as if questioning his authority as a storyteller. The tale did not end the way the narrator had led me to expect.

But Ngandi is not daunted. Listen carefully to Kenyatta's words in the court: "Our activities have been against the injustices suffered by the African people . . . What we have done, and what we shall continue to do, is to demand the rights of the African people as human beings that they may enjoy the facilities and privileges in the same way as other people." Do you think he was just talking to Prosecutor Somerhough and Judge Thacker? What would be the point? His words are a signal to Mbiyũ and Kĩmathi to continue and intensify the struggle. He will be free for greater glory: Remember that Kenyatta's friend Kwame Nkrumah came from prison when he became a prime minister of Gold Coast only a year ago, 1951. PG, prison graduate, he called himself. And Nehru? Was he not a prison graduate?

I note how in time the main characters in his story change: It is now Field Marshall Dedan Kĩmathi, his generals, their guerrilla army, who are the movers of history. I ask Ngandi why one of them is called General China. He does not hesitate. He tells me a little about the Chinese liberating themselves in 1948, a year after India's independence, but he does not elaborate. I ask him about rumors I had heard that black Americans and black South Africans would come to help us.

South Africans and black Americans have their own struggles. But they are sympathetic to our plight, Ngandi tells me. Bishop Alexander from South Africa was here, a guest of KISA and Karĩng'a, between 1935 and 1937, to help ordain clergy of the Orthodox faith, such as Arthur G. Gatũng'ũ of Waithaka. Black Americans have already been involved in our fight. He mentions Marcus Garvey, whose journal, *Negro World*, somehow reached KCA leaders in the 1920s. And after the Kenya settlers and the colonial state massacred those demanding the release of Harry Thuku in 1922, Marcus Garvey himself called a huge rally at Liberty Hall in New York, and on their behalf sent a telegram to Lloyd George and prophesied that in thirty years Kenyans would wage armed struggle against the British. Marcus Garvey was a prophet. What he said has come to be. He cites the friendship of Kenyatta with Paul Robeson, George Padmore, and W. E. B. Dubois and the 1945 Pan-African Congress in Manchester. Ralph Bunche, a big man in the United Nations, was Chief Koinange's friend. Mbiyũ was educated in America and he must have made many friends. But the soldiers who came to Kenya Teachers' College at Gĩthũngũri in 1944 and sang Negro spirituals may have been behind the talk of black Americans coming to help us fight the British. He reminds us that Mbiyũ is free, abroad, who knows? Everything comes back to Mbiyũ, the genius, though Kĩmathi, the general, is increasingly occupying center stage.

It is Kĩmathi who will set Kenyatta free. To lull skeptical eyes and ears Ngandi tells the story of how Dedan Kĩmathi once disguised himself as a white police officer and went to dine with the governor, sending him a letter of thanks afterward. He tells of other more amazing feats: how Kĩmathi can crawl on his belly for miles and miles; how he makes his enemies think they have seen him, but before they can pull out their guns they don't see him, they see a leopard glaring at them before leaping into the bush. This side of Kĩmathi is the more appealing to my imagination, and I want to hear more about his spectacular feats.

I am amazed by the extent of Ngandi's knowledge—Gĩthũngũri must have been a really good college—but even more so by how freely Ngandi can move from the natural to the supernatural and back without batting an eyelid. Fact or fiction or both, Mzee Ngandi makes sense of it all, in his matter-of-fact tone and with his occasional irony, not to mention his whistling to himself.

Years later, in my novel *Weep Not, Child* I would give to the young fictional Njoroge an aura of fact and rumor, certainty and doubt, despair and hope, but I am not sure if I was able truly to capture the intricate web of the mundane and the dramatic, the surreal normality of ordinary living under extraordinary times in a country at war. In the facts and rumors of the trial and imprisonment of Jomo Kenyatta and the heroic exploits of Dedan Kĩmathi, the real and the surreal were one. Perhaps it is myth as much as fact that keeps dreams alive even in times of war.

I am sending word to your father that you are now ready to become a man, my mother tells me toward the end of 1953, the first time she has spoken to me about my father since she left his house years ago. Both parents must give consent to this rite of passage. But I am entering this rite, at this time, in obedience to a voice from the grave. My grandmother's last words were clear: Ndũng'ũ, Kĩmũchũ's son, must not leave me behind. So the date is tied to Ndũng'ũ's choice of when he will be ready for the rite of passage. Fortunately, the time chosen coincides with the school vacation at the end of the year.

In precolonial times, circumcision among the Gĩkũyũ marked the passage to adulthood. In a society where governance, military obligations, law, and morality presupposed the succession of generations, this rite was a necessary stage up the ladder of social life, for the balance and continuity of the whole. The entire ceremony—the preparation, the act, and the healing—was therefore communal, familial, and personal at the same time. In olden times, the dates would have been set by a council of elders for the whole nation. The candidates, young men and women, would go through the three stages at about the same time. All the initiated during that period would comprise the class of that particular year, and they would be given a name that would forever remain unique to them. The age group would also be on a par with family and clan in terms of personal identity and expectations of loyalty. But loyalty to one's age group was stronger because it cut across families, clans, and regions.

That was why Mbiyũ Koinange could use age group loyalty as a mobilizing tool for funding the Kenya Teachers' College at Gĩthũngũri. But in colonial society the organization of power was based on different legal criteria, covering as it did a multiplicity of nations, each of which had ordered its precolonial life according to particular cultural traditions. So, even for Gĩkũyũ people, circumcision in my time no longer played the political, economic, and legal role in the community that it once did. It neither conferred special communally sanctioned rights nor demanded special communally set obligations and expectations. In my time, only remnants of the rite's communal past remained. Many males, even those not religiously affiliated, drifted to hospitals for the surgery. I would not be one of them. I wanted to go through it. I hoped it would contribute to my self-identity and the sense of belonging that I had always sought.

Of the three stages, before, during, and after the act, I find the preparatory more enjoyable: It is carnival time with house-to-house performances. In olden days the celebration would have moved from village to village, region to region, limited to distances that could be traveled on foot. My sisters and brothers from my father's and my mother's houses have been here, helping to cook and do other chores, and most have stayed for the special night of Mararanja, the eve of the rite, when hardly anybody sleeps.

I have seen this before, when it involved others, because everybody, adult, child, man, and woman, can take part in the dancing and singing. But it is not as easy to lose oneself in the festival when one is a candidate for the knife. Besides, my voice has now broken and lost its quality. I used to sing set pieces with set words, but the singing in our house is now a strict call-and-response affair with often unexpected challenges directed at the candidates. It is lyric improvisation within a set melody. The candidate has to be alert, creative, and prompt, but fortunately one can be aided by those who are more able, and my relatives are there to help me. Some of the challenges are erotic in nature; in fact all the dances and songs contain lewd verses and suggestive hip motions. It is a period of license to talk sex but not to engage in it. Boundaries are drawn strictly between mime and reality. Satiric verses alternate with vulgar abuses and equally vulgar responses ending in reconciliatory tender lyrical words. The whole night is a musical feast of melody after melody, dance after dance, with a constant to and fro of human traffic between our house and Ndũng'ũ's place.

I enjoy all this but I am thinking about the knife cutting through the flesh. I am also thinking about my friend Kenneth. I don't know the details, but a family conflict prevents unanimity about his candidacy. Ndũng'ũ and I will leave him behind. I feel sorry for him and all my mates, because after tomorrow I cannot play with them anymore for it would be like an adult playing with children. The gulf that opens between initiates and noninitiates is abrupt, deep, and wide and cannot be bridged by any means other than undergoing the rite.

At long last the morning of the event arrives. I have not slept at all. But still I am ordered to wake up very early for the *menjo,* the ceremony of shaving off head and pubic hair. First I have to take off my clothes, an enactment of shedding childhood. The shorn hair is buried in the ground, symbolizing the burial of that stage of my life. I remain naked as now we move on to the Manguo waters. It is a long way there, it seems to me, although in reality it is only one and a half miles. Men, women, and children are following, jostling, dancing, and singing, some waving green leaves in the air. By the time all the candidates meet at the waters, the procession of supporters has become a massive crowd, milling about.

Suddenly at the water ceremony there is a surprise. Kenneth Mbũgua has been allowed to participate after all. His parents have decided that there was no way that we, his playmates and schoolmates, would leave him behind. But there was no time to shave him, so he is the only candidate with head and pubic hair. I am glad to see him, but there is no time to talk. We are being shepherded toward our fate.

The water is extremely cold, chilly, but now again I am thinking of the knife. Shall I be able to endure the pain and come out of it with courage? I know there is concern in my camp. Cowardice is defined very narrowly. If I so much as blink or let out the slightest sound or make the faintest facial expression, I shall bring shame to my family and community and the word "coward" will stick, a stigma for life. The candidates are a mixture of those who have been to school and those who have not. Students are looked upon as having been softened by books and modern learning. They cannot take pain. I know that the eyes of the curious are on me.

Each of us has a guardian. Mine is my half brother Njinjũ wa Njeri, the third son of the fourth of my father's wives. Yongĩ is Ndũng'ũ's guardian. I am not sure about Kenneth's, but, really, now, as I am made to sit down on the grass, I am worrying only about my own fate. My legs are open, knees bent, firmly planted on the ground. My hands form fists, thumb between the middle and index finger, my elbows rest on my knees. My manhood is there for all to stare at, but in reality they are not interested in it; they are more concerned with my reaction when the knife meets the foreskin. I hear some movement. It is the surgeon. My guardian is standing behind me holding me down by the shoulders. I remain completely frozen: Oh, Lord, let me go through this without flinching. During the preparations some people have been telling us scary tales, of the knife accidentally cutting too deeply or even slicing off a piece of one's manhood. I don't believe it but suppose . . . suppose something went wrong? I don't know the surgeon; I have heard that my relative Mwangi Karuithia might officiate. I don't even see the surgeon's face. It is over before I know it is happening. I do not feel the knife. The cold water had numbed my skin. My guardian quickly covers me with a white cotton cloth that extends from my shoulders to my feet; all the women are ululating with pride. I know I have come through. So do Ndũng'ũ and Kenneth. After the surgery one can express pain in any way, even through tears; there is now no stigma attached to such reactions, but I try to hold myself together. I must not contribute to the view, which I don't accept, that book learning makes one soft and weak.

We walk back. The sides of our white togas are held together by a line of safety pins. The Gĩkũyũ don't remove the foreskin completely, it is left hanging below the tip of the penis. I have been taught how to walk, legs apart, one hand holding up the penis, a finger separating the tip from the hanging foreskin, so that it does not rub against the loose foreskin or against the cloth. The walk is difficult and slow. The entourage that had escorted us to the waterside has largely disappeared, no doubt to catch up with sleep and neglected tasks.

We three, Kenneth, Ndũng'ũ, and I, end up in the healing shed, a small hut, deep in my grandfather's land, but not too near any compound. We, the initiates, lie on beds of straw, covered with sheets and blankets. Kenneth has a mentor, Karanja Zinguri. Our three mentors sleep in a room opposite, with a common living space between us. But we can hear them, and they can hear us. No initiate is allowed to go back to his normal life at home. We are set apart. We shall be kept here for three weeks at least. Food will be brought to us, but not even relatives are allowed beyond the door without permission from the guardians. During the healing period, our three guardians are our only contact with the world. They are our mentors, guides, and instructors in the ways of adulthood and manly responsibilities.

Though they are concerned with our physical welfare, our mentors are also training us in the ways of self-control. Questions about our swollen foreskin, which looks tumorous, elicit from them the horrifying response that we are growing a second penis. If I had known that the rite involved having two . . . but I do not want to contemplate such an outcome. They occasionally bring in girls to simulate the sex act, an exaggerated performance of lovemaking with erotic noises meant to reach our ears. This results in our tumescence, stretching the healing skin, causing excruciating pain, till one of us screams, Stop! Stop it. They come out laughing, lecturing us about self-control. My fear of the predicted "growth" of a second penis ends only after the foreskin becomes simply a soft growth below the tip of the penis. And now they tell us about the healed foreskin. It is good for the woman; it massages her nicely, and that is why it is called *ngwati*, "lovemaker," partner in love motions.

Afterward, when we heal enough to walk without too much pain, we shall be allowed to socialize with other initiates from the other villages before returning to our shed to sleep. Other initiates can also visit us. All the initiates are still identifiable by our uniform: a long togalike cloth fastened by safety pins. A bamboo walking stick completes the attire. When we walk along the road, people of all ages give way.

Eventually the day comes when we are given back our regular clothes, say farewell to our shed and mentors, and go home to our everyday life, with a difference. I am now a man. I belong to a new age group. I have cut off all social links with friends who have not undergone this rite. I cannot socialize with them, play with them, share secrets with them. Our contacts and conversations are minimal and formal. It is as if I had jumped over an invisible wall from one side of life to another. On the other side of the wall is my old self; on this side, the new. I am now welcome into the social company of my elder brother Wallace and his friends. I can attend their parties and be privy to their jokes and stories about women.

Kahanya, my brother's close friend, takes me under his wing and eases my path into the company of men. He introduces me to the girl with whom I will soon lose my virginity, the last rite of entry into the new world. It is not a great moment, but it is the proof I need that I have become a man indeed.

Though the whole ritual of becoming a man leaves a deep impression on me, I emerge from it convinced more deeply that, for our times, education and learning, not a mark on the flesh, are the way to empower men and women.

We returned to Kĩnyogori Intermediate School, a two-year middle school between elementary and secondary school, but we would be there for only one year, having spent the other year at the old Manguo site, awaiting completion of new buildings at the new location. The school was under the Kĩambu District Education Board. This was going to be the third move of my elementary school career.

It was 1954, a pivotal year, the last stage of my primary education, at the end of which I would take the Kenya African Preliminary Exams, a make-or-break educational rite of passage. There were corresponding exams for Asians and Europeans for entry into equally racially segregated secondary schools. Integration was not a central demand in anticolonial politics, except for the general call to end the color bar. School integration would come about later, after independence in 1963. The chief demands were for land and freedom, and equal opportunity in educational facilities. For Africans, there were very few secondary schools, and the competition to attend these was extremely fierce, many students falling by the wayside. The situation worsened after the closure of independent schools and the Kenya Teachers'

College at Gĩthũngũri. The Beecher Report, which sought
to streamline and expand African secondary schooling, was
out of tune with the needs of the times even before it came
out, and competition intensified.

For us, the challenges were not purely academic or confined to the school compound. There was the simple one of
distance: Kĩnyogori was six miles away. Harder challenges
involved tuition and uniforms, as usual. The long walk to
school provided an opportunity for news and entertainment:
We swapped stories about what had happened in our homes
and neighborhoods. The state of emergency had acquired
the dimensions of a huge mysterious creature, ever growing
as it trod menacingly toward us. Everybody had a tale to tell
of what it had done to their family, neighbors, or relatives in
Nairobi—victims of its operations from Jock Scott to General Erskine's Operation Anvil that sought to remove all
members of Gĩkũyũ, Embu, and Meru communities from
Nairobi. The creature became the instrument of what was
now the official colonial policy: the dislocation of thousands.
Limuru was only about eighteen miles from the capital.
There were stories of the dead, and of hundreds herded into
concentration camps. Of course, some stories were about
how so-and-so had managed to slip through the net, but
most were about the desolation the state of emergency had
wrought.

In the villages, tales spread of how some avoided compliance with forced communal labor and compulsory *baraza*
attendance: of how fathers or mothers had locked themselves inside stinking latrines and yet had been ferreted out

by the Home Guards; others who faked illnesses or death to
no avail; and yet others who hid in holes they had dug, covering them to look like their surroundings. It was clear that the
constant daytime and nighttime raids and the mass incarcer-
ations were breaking up families, taking away or incapacitat-
ing breadwinners, and diminishing parental care. People
lived under a double fear: of government operations by day
and Mau Mau guerrilla activities by night, the difference
being that while the guerrillas were fighting for land and
freedom, the colonial state was fighting to sustain foreign
occupation and protect the prerogatives and wealth of European settlers.

The British day raids, aided by loyalist Home Guard
squads, were often sudden and unexpected. They would
quickly surround and cordon off the Limuru market. Those
netted would be made to squat in twos, threes, or fours, depending on the size of the crowd, their hands held together
behind their necks, while they were guarded on all sides by
armed British forces of white officers and black policemen.
They would stay in that torturous position under the hot
sun awaiting screening. One by one they would walk past a
table occupied by a British armed officer. Beside him would
be one or two hooded men, called *gakũnia*, who would nod
yes or no to the person's involvement in Mau Mau. A yes
nod meant further questioning for the culprit and then on to
a concentration camp. These mass screenings were dreaded,
and when the army trucks were sighted, word would pass
swiftly. Many young men would abandon their jobs and go
into hiding or run away, sometimes under intense machine-

gun fire. I would listen to these episodes, pondering the bad that had not yet happened to my mother's house and counting my blessings. There were near misses. There was one incident the memory of which I always tried to suppress.

It happened months before I became a man. School was then still at Manguo. I don't know what possessed me and made me run home for a lunch I was not sure I would find. My mother and my sister Njoki, sitting outside in the yard sorting out some beans they would later cook, were surprised to see me at that hour, and, predictably, there was nothing to calm my hunger. My mother offered to roast some potatoes, the only thing available, but this would take hours, and I would miss school or else be very late. I looked up wistfully at the unripe fruits on the pear tree. She never allowed us to pick unripe fruits; she said this interfered with the rhythm of life of the plant, and she did not want to hurt its feelings. But this time she did not object, although she never nodded consent. After eating I dashed in the hut, took some water, and ran out into the yard, ready to go back to school.

It was my mother who suddenly became aware of people surreptitiously running through the surrounding cornfields. She shouted at me to come back. Seeing my hesitation, she reminded me that it was she who had struck the pact with me and it was she who was telling me to break it. Hungry and frustrated, despite the unripe pears, I ignored her plea and continued walking down the path by the hedge that divided our land from Kahahu's estate. I had not gone far when I heard gunfire. Silence. Then at a distance I saw them, many Johnnies, as the British soldiers were called, spread out in the fields everywhere. I hid behind a blue gum tree and slowly started walking back, hoping the tree would shield me from view. Then I heard more gunfire. Screams and shouts. Gunfire. I fell down, started crawling on all fours, before getting up and running back home. My mother and sister, who were still standing in the yard, dragged me into the hut. We could still hear sounds of gunfire, but after a time they faded into silence, and the Johnnies did not come anywhere near our home. I was shaken but relieved that I had not walked straight into the path of the gunfire. It was probably the first time I had failed to go to school for reasons other than illness.

When in the evening Wallace and his friends came home, they were full of talk of how each had escaped. There were many who had been taken away for questioning and to concentration camps. They talked of rumors of death, but they were not sure of the victims or even whether this was only one of the many tales that accompanied every raid. It was clear that this was not the first time my brother and his friends had run away from raids at the marketplace.

A few days later we learned that some people had been killed, one of the casualties being Gĩtogo, my half brother, the last born of Wangarĩ's sons. His case was tragic. Gĩtogo worked in a butchery in Limuru. He had started running, following the example of others. Being deaf, he did not hear the white officer shouting *simama*, stop. They shot him in the back.

His death exemplified what was beginning to happen to

families everywhere. Gĩtogo was the younger brother of Joseph Kabae, ex-military man, the owner of a legal and secretarial services firm, who was now working for the colonial state, one of the few who were licensed to carry a pistol, though he was always dressed in civilian clothes.

I remembered Gĩtogo as a regular jovial presence at the storytelling sessions at his mother's hut, despite the fact that he could not hear. A handsome youth, Gĩtogo had a winning personality and never did any harm to anybody. He was always ready to come to the aid of all, particularly when it came to lifting heavy loads. I was sad to hear of his death. But since we had lived apart from my father's house for some years, Gĩtogo's death, though painful, may not have hit me as directly as it had others who were in daily contact with him.

By the time I went through the ceremony of becoming a man and resumed schooling at Kĩnyogori, the memory of this tragedy had faded. A human normalizes the unusual in order to survive. I could still count my blessings because though the state-of-emergency creature had now touched my father's house, it had not yet reached the compound of my mother's house.

If anything, there was a happy addition there. Wallace had gotten married to the beautiful girl guide from Banana Hills, Charity Wanjikũ, and they were blessed with Mũturi, their first child. It was interesting to see Wallace, the efficient carpenter, become a family man, a tender father, always anxious to come home to his wife, gazing at the newborn as if he could not believe that he was their flesh and blood. Before the birth of his son, he still lived the bachelor life he was used to, sometimes spending the night in his workshop or elsewhere with his peers. But now we saw him almost every night, which also made us feel more secure and united as a family.

Military vehicles, raids, screenings, screams, sirens from the Home Guard post, the sounds of machine-gun fire were becoming part of daily life. They made me feel that the slouching creature was inexorably closing in on my mother's house.

Yet when it finally struck on that April day in 1954, I was completely unprepared for it.

Good Wallace was a member of the supply wing of the nationalist guerrilla army, the Kenya Land and Freedom Army. He and Uncle Gĩcini arranged to meet with a friendly source that would supply them with bullets. The source was the brother of a girl my brother used to date, but they had parted amicably. The meeting was in the open by a road that linked the old Indian shops to the African marketplace. Between my mother's parcel of land and the road was a small hedge. At the time, my mother was tending a mixed crop of green corn and beans. Good Wallace and Uncle Gĩcini shouted greetings to her. Otherwise she was unbothered by the goings-on in the busy road. Twelve bullets and money exchanged hands and the source went away. Wallace and Gĩcini divided the bullets between them, six each. Wallace put his share in the inner pocket of his jacket, Uncle Gĩcini, in his trouser pockets.

Uncle Gĩcini and my brother had not moved a step when a police truck suddenly appeared and stopped them. Unaware that their source was an informer, they took this to be the usual police harassment that was so common at the time. They thought they would be able to talk or even bribe their way out of trouble. The policeman assigned to frisk them started with my brother, going through every pocket except the one that contained the bullets. Then he went over to Uncle Gĩcini and found six bullets in his pocket. While the police concentrated entirely on Uncle Gĩcini, my brother dipped his hand in the inner pocket, took out the bullets, and threw them over the hedge onto the side where my mother was cultivating. The police were aware of the number of bullets that had changed hands, yet they found only six. Puzzled, the same policeman left Gĩcini in handcuffs and came back to frisk my brother again, this time not forgetting the inner pocket. Again he found nothing on him.

The two of them were going to be taken to the police station anyway for further questioning but were treated differently. The apparently more dangerous Gĩcini was placed in the front passenger seat, handcuffed, sandwiched between two armed officers. My brother was hurled in the back of the truck, without handcuffs, guarded by one officer only. By this time the fracas had attracted the attention of my mother, who looked over the hedge. My brother told her not to worry; he would be all right. She should simply *thikĩrĩra mbembe icio wega*. This phrase had two meanings. The most common was simply a call for her to cover the stems of the growing corn with mulch. But it could also mean to bury grains of corn under the soil. *Mbembe* was a secret Mau Mau code for "bullets." So it could also mean "hide the bullets carefully." The law in those days was clear: Anybody caught with bullets was hanged at Gĩthũngũri, the former Kenya Teachers' College.

Good Wallace decided to escape. He jumped off the truck onto the road and then fled through the Indian shops, bullets whistling behind him, an escape that set in motion various narratives, like the version I heard on that day as I came home from Kĩnyogori.

The real narrative emerged later over time. On that night my mother offered no details of her role or presence at the time of Good Wallace's arrest. My brother's wife, who held their firstborn in her arms, was also mum, torn no doubt by conflicting emotions. My brother's escape may have become instant legend, but for my mother, for his new bride and their child, for us, it was just a relief. He had escaped with his life intact. But we were also suspended between fear and hope. Would he survive the manhunt? And life in the mountains? But we did not voice our fears or hopes or anything else even to ourselves. We simply sat huddled around the fireside, shadows and light playing on our faces. My mother was the only one who spoke, taking us all in as she told us to watch our lips. The dreaded state of emergency had finally struck my mother's house.

I was never to let anybody know that we knew where Good Wallace had gone because, indeed, in a technical sense, we did not. Do you hear me? she asked again rhetorically, looking at my younger brother and me. If anybody asks if you know where he is, just say, I don't know.

I don't have to be told. I know it inside me. It is strange that when I wake up in the morning, everything looks the same: the sky, the land, the neighborhood. And yet everything has changed. Tomorrow when I go to school, or read a newspaper, or talk with Mzee Ngandi and hear of Mau Mau and their heroic deeds or deaths, the talk will not be something abstract, happening far away in the forest of Nyandarwa and Mount Kenya. I will be thinking of my brother whom I have loved: his hard work, his determination, his imagination, his love and loyalty to friends. I will be thinking of Joseph Kabae, who had earlier taught Good Wallace how to type, and now teacher and student are on opposite sides of the conflict. Yes, I will be thinking of the split in my father's house with two of Wangarĩ's sons, Tumbo and Kabae, working as agents of the colonial state and their half brother out in the mountains trying to bring down the colonial state. Ah, yes, brothers who love one another, now at war.

The story is told of how my brother Wallace once went to visit Mwangi wa Gacoki, the son of the second wife of my father. Wa Gacoki then worked at the Limuru Bata Shoe factory and lived in one of the company's single-room houses. By one of those coincidences of fate, Tumbo, the informer, Wangarĩ's eldest son and the brother to Kabae, had decided to visit Mwangi wa Gacoki at the same hour. When they encountered one another at the gate, they both took off in different directions—Good Wallace back to the mountains and my half brother Tumbo to the police station. Soon there was a large sweep of the area. But obviously Tumbo did not mention wa Gacoki because he was never called in for questioning about the incident or accused of aiding an anti-colonial guerrilla fighter. Or maybe Tumbo did not know that Wallace was going to visit Mwangi wa Gacoki, since the workers' quarters were many and crowded. Warring motives and loyalties might have been at play.

And yet the split loyalties do not break the sense of us belonging to the same family. My mother's co-wives don't abandon her; they still find the time to see her at home or in the fields. But I assume that they don't talk about Kabae or Tumbo or my brother. Or perhaps they know, deep inside, that these warring sons would always be their sons, and they hope that all of them will eventually come back home safely. The Gĩkũyũ have a saying that out of the same womb comes both a killer and a healer.

My brother's flight to the mountains changes our external relationship to our immediate world. But I learn it the hard way. At first, neither my brother's wife nor I can believe it. It seems impossible but Kahanya, the closest friend of my brother, the man he had taught carpentry and employed as his assistant at the workshop, has joined the Home Guards. No, it is not possible that Kahanya would join those who were hunting down my brother. It is not possible that the man who had married a girl from one of the most militantly anticolonial families, the Kĩhĩkas, would turn against what his in-laws stand for. No, Kahanya whose elder brother, Ndereba Karanja, had married Nyagaki, Gacoki's daughter, one of my older half sisters, would not turn against us. I refuse to believe it.

One day I encounter Kahanya wearing the white armband identifying him as a Home Guard. He is in the company of another Home Guard, Gĩkonyo Marinda, also one of my brother's age-mates. The encounter takes place on the path that then passed by Edward Matumbĩ's house, and on either side of which grew long green corn. I almost freeze. They both stop. Gĩkonyo glares at me as if I am contaminated with evil. But Kahanya, though not looking at me directly, greets me and then asks, Does Good Wallace ever get in touch with you? I say no, which is the truth anyway. He tells me mockingly, almost jeeringly, We understand your brother has climbed to the ranks of captain. I don't know, I say, and continue on my way, and they continue on theirs, laughing. Both, I later understood, had taken the oath as Mau Mau adherents. They had simply changed sides. How do I make sense of these contradictions in a struggle, which, through Ngandi's rendering, I had seen as one between the anticolonial and the colonial, good and evil? What is now emerging around me is murky.

One morning I go to my grandfather's as I was used to doing. Even though I am now a man, I am still his scribe and bird of good omen. He does not mention my brother's flight to the mountains, but I note that he is not as enthusiastic about the early-morning call as he used to be. On another occasion he tells me that I need not visit him anymore so early in the morning. A third visit in broad daylight: He makes it clear that I am no longer his bird of good omen at whatever time of day. I am his beloved scribe no more.

At first I am hurt. He is my mother's father; I am named after him; once he had hidden in our place in the dark. But that was the point, really. Grandfather had already lost Kĩmũchũ, his beloved adopted son, and now he might lose

Gĩcini, his own blood. His grandson, the son of his daughter who lived on his land, is a Mau Mau guerrilla. I am sad to lose my special place as his scribe and bird of good omen, but somehow I understand. My mother's house has become a menace to others.

But ours remains a close-knit one-parent family. In addition to the comfort my mother's house gives me, there is school. Though the fear that I might lose my place in Kĩnyogori hovers over me always, it does not actually happen. I am grateful. I seek refuge in learning.

There were many primary school teachers who, in their own ways, contributed to my intellectual growth. But the one who most influenced my life was Mr. Samuel G. Kĩbicho. He graduated from Kagumo Teacher Training College. He became the headmaster of the newly reopened Manguo, and it was under his leadership that the school moved to Kĩnyogori. He was my English teacher during my last two years at Manguo and Kĩnyogori.

Our language texts from grade five were the *Oxford Readers for Africa*. The books featured two characters, John and Joan, who lived in Oxford but went to school in Reading. I learned that they went by train, which triggered envy in me. Of course, Oxford was in England. I don't think that any of our teachers had ever been there, so the places mentioned in the texts must have been as strange to them as they were to us. We followed Joan and John everywhere, especially to London, where they went sightseeing at natural, historical, and architectural landmarks including the Thames, the British Houses of Parliament with Big Ben, and Westminster Abbey. The school now followed the common government syllabus for African schools, so the teachers had to use the officially sanctioned texts. Mr. Kĩbicho had the ability to go outside the texts and cite many everyday examples from our environment. He was excellent with English grammar. He made me understand the structure of the language and how to use simple and complex sentences or how to build a sentence of ever increasing complexity from a simple one. From the simple to the complex: It was an outlook that remained imprinted in my mind. If that was all he did, he would have remained just like any other good teacher in my life.

But he had literary texts in his personal library. I don't know how he noted my interest in reading, but he gave me the simplified Dickens's *Great Expectations*, which I passed on to Kenneth. Then Kenneth borrowed from him *Lorna Doone* by Richard Doddridge Blackmore, and passed it on to me. One had to return the book that one had borrowed before one was allowed to take another. By exchanging what we borrowed, between Kenneth and me, we always had two books at any given time. We became avid readers and we talked about what we read. Of all the books that we read, the most gripping and memorable was Robert Louis Stevenson's *Treasure Island*. Whereas the others were abridged, this one was not or only slightly so. We kept on borrowing it over and over again. Kenneth and I talked about it, the story, the characters, especially Long John Silver and his parrot. I identified with Jim Hawkins, his hopes and fears, his ingenuity, his narrow escapes. We memorized certain phrases and songs:

Fifteen men on the dead man's chest
Yo-ho-ho, and a bottle of rum
Drink and the devil had done the rest
Yo-ho-ho, and a bottle of rum.

Sometimes, in the schoolyard, Kenneth and I would recite "Yo-ho-ho" to the surprise, bafflement, and curiosity of other students. We discussed the possibility of our going to sea to become pirates, but alas there was nothing beyond rivers and Manguo marshes in Limuru, and Mombasa was very far away.

It was Stevenson who provoked my first major literary dispute. I confided to Kenneth that I would like to write stories like Stevenson's, but that one needed a license to write. And to qualify to write, one had to have higher education. Kenneth was adamant that one did not need to have a license to write, or any other qualification. I countered by asserting that if one wrote without such permission, one would surely be arrested. I don't know why this idea of being imprisoned because of one's writing came to my mind. Perhaps in my conversations with Mzee Ngandi, he had mentioned the fact that many of the nationalist writers, like Gakaara Wanjaũ, Mũgĩa, and Stanley Kagĩka, had been imprisoned by the colonial state under the laws of the state of emergency. African-language papers had been banned, and some of the editors, such as Henry Muoria of *Mũmenyereri*, were forced into exile. Whatever the origins of my position, the debate between Kenneth and me was quite heated at times.

We could have resolved it easily by posing the problem to Mr. Kĩbicho, but we did not.

Irritated by my intransigence, Kenneth said that he would write a book to prove to me that one did not need a state license to write. He did not tell me what the book would be about or whether he had started. But he could not have gone very far. Our attention was soon taken up with preparations for the Kenya African Preliminary Exams, which would decide our fate.

The Kenya African Preliminary Exams were dreaded. Only about 5 percent of the students taking the tests ever found places at high schools or teacher training colleges. Preparing for the exams was nerve-racking, made more so by our being in the midst of a war. We were continually deprived of sleep by interruptions at unexpected times, and I was always wondering about my brother in the mountains. How to prepare for the exams was a problem. Were the questions going to be based on one year's work, on the previous two, three, or four years of work? Except for English, we did not have textbooks. We depended on the teachers' notes that we had copied from the blackboard. There were very few students if any who would have been able to preserve in one place notes taken over a period of one year.

But I tried reading time and again whatever notes I had. Even that was a struggle. Some days we were without paraffin for the lamp. I had to read by firelight. Dry cornstalks could produce sudden bright flames but the flames also died as quickly. One had to keep on feeding the flames. It was a race to read as much as one could within the span of one set of flames. It strained my eyes but I got used to it. Daylight was best. But reading had to compete with chores, including looking for firewood for the evening.

The exams were a very formal affair. They were often held at one center with the candidates from different schools finding their own way to the place. In 1954, for our area the center was at Loreto Convent School, Limuru, three miles from home. We felt lucky because there were some who had to travel more than ten miles to get there, and there was hardly any transportation.

The Catholic mission where Loreto School was located had been founded by Italian missionaries in 1906. The vast land the church owned was part of Tigoni, the center of the dispute that eventually led to the Lari massacre in 1953. But although there was a saying that there was no difference between a priest and a settler, the anger of the population was directed more at soldier settlements than at the mission center itself.

A week or so before the exams, I was awakened from deep sleep by my mother opening the door. A group of men entered the house. They wore long coats, and at the waist were belts from which swords in leather sheaths hung. A few had guns slung over their shoulders. One of them was smiling at me. I could not believe my eyes. It was my elder brother, Good Wallace, alive and smiling, holding a flashlight in his hand. By this time, his wife, her baby in tow, had come in from her house. I was trembling with a mix of fear and joy. He was alive and well. But what if Home Guards were following them? These men showed no fear. They were talking freely, though in low voices, and even laughing. They ate food and drank some tea. They must have had sentries outside because there was always some movement in and out. Then my brother turned to me and said, Don't fear. I know you will be taking exams soon. I came to wish you good luck. As our mother says, try your best. Knowledge is our light. And they left. Just like that. My mother impressed upon me that what I had seen was not to be discussed with anybody else. Not even my younger brother, who had slept through it all. In the morning I thought that I was waking up from a strange dream.

I was sorry that I could not have asked all the questions on my mind: about the day he had escaped death, the way they lived in the mountains, the battles they had fought, or about their leader Marshall Dedan Kĩmathi. But the thought that my elder brother would risk being caught so as to wish me good luck was very touching. He was the same person who used to discourage me from playing with carpenter tools but whose face beamed bright when I was absorbed in a book or a newspaper. His risky visit motivated me to work harder, but it also added to my anxiety.

My anxiety became sheer panic when, almost a week or so later, Joseph Kabae, the king's man, turned up in our house. He smelled of alcohol but was his affable self. It was early in the evening. He had a belt from which hung a holstered gun. He was passing by and, remembering that he had never come to visit, he thought he would stop in just to ask, How are you? he explained. My mother made him a cup of tea, but there was not much flow of words between stepmother and stepson. I was sure of the thoughts in my mother's head:

Why so soon after Good Wallace's visit by night? The questions I always had now came back: Why was this man, who had fought white people in the Second World War, not out in the mountains fighting against the white settlers? Then suddenly he turned to me: You are about to take exams, I know. Don't fear the exams. They are just words on paper; attack them with the pen. The pen is your weapon. Then he took out his gun from the holster and held it in front of my face. He wanted me to touch it, maybe to drive out the fear in me, but I didn't. My mother's eyes were cold with disapproval, and there was a discernible collective sigh of relief when he left. His visit so soon after that of Wallace left a cloud of fear and anxiety: In taking out his gun, was Kabae showing off or conveying a message? It was notable that he never mentioned the brother in the mountains. I took it in the most positive light: He was the most highly educated in our family; maybe he was genuinely coming to wish me well. The guerrilla and the king's soldier had both come to say almost identical words to me.

The eve of the exams brought back the kind of fear and anxiety that I had felt on the eve of circumcision. It was the fear of the unknown, where the consequences of failure were clear but those of success were not. Now there would not be any direct communal involvement, just me and my notebooks. There was the three-mile walk to Loreto, and I was hoping that I would get there on time.

I had never been to Loreto Convent School, though I had seen its students in passing. The day I would have gone there, to convert to Catholicism, I was turned away by Kenneth's mother. And now, at long last, I was there, though for a different purpose. The contrast with Kĩnyogori was remarkable. The buildings, from the church to the classrooms, were surrounded by lots of land, with well-mowed grass and well-trimmed hedges. Farther out were paddocks with cows, their udders full, grazing peacefully. The classrooms were joined by corridors in which one could have gotten lost, but some girls had been assigned to guide us to the exam room. And wonder of wonders: They had toilets that one flushed after use, and the waste would disappear. Ours at Kĩnyogori and earlier at Manguo were pit latrines. The girls told us that they had shower rooms too. In everything, their style of life was far above ours. I could not recall a more intimidating environment.

But most dazzling were the school uniforms—red dresses, so colorful in contrast with our drab khaki. I could not keep my eyes off the girls: They all looked equally beautiful, intelligent, radiant, sinless, ready to be received into a heavenly choir of angels. One or two nuns in their habits hovered. I don't know what was more daunting, the school environment as a whole, or the room where we sat behind desks, spaced in such a manner as to make it impossible to cast an eye on our neighbor's answer sheets. The proctor was a white education officer from Nairobi who, after preliminary instructions, sat in front but would sometimes walk between the rows to ensure that there was no cheating. The exams took four days to complete. On the first, there was registration, orientation, and the assignment of a number in lieu of one's name. The other three were each devoted to one or two subjects, including math, English, Swahili, history, geography, and civics. I was nervous, almost paralyzed, as I looked at each exam in front of me and at the girls in red, who seemed at ease with themselves. But the moment I put pen to paper I felt a kind of animated serenity. Every day brought the same anxieties and the same attempts to calm my emotions, and then serenity. On the English exam I had an unexpected encounter with my recent past. Among the questions was a passage meant to test our comprehension. Read this and answer the following questions. The passage was taken from Stevenson's *Treasure Island*. The passage did not contain the title of the book or the author's name. But it had signature lines and phrases: "Fifteen men on the dead man's chest / Yo-ho-ho, and a bottle of rum." It was probably incomprehensible to many candidates, who complained about it afterward, but for Kenneth and me, who understood the context, it was a reward for our extracurricular readings.

By the fourth and last day I was exhausted in body and mind. It was a relief when it was all over.

Over, too, for me, were my years at Kĩnyogori. The struggle for school from Kamandũra School, through Manguo Karĩng'a, to Kĩnyogori Intermediate, a government school; the ups and downs in the fortune of my mother's house; the drums of war in the country—any of these events could have derailed me from my educational track. Now it was time to say good-bye to the school and the history it carried. Sadly, it was also time to say good-bye to Mr. Kĩbicho and his library.

The weeks of waiting for exam results were among the longest of my life. We were not under the protective umbrella of a school any longer. We were subject to the same perpetual rhythm of tension bedeviling the entire population. Now and then my mother was called to the Home Guard post for questioning. Apparently somebody had revealed the other meaning of *mbembe*. But my mother was always consistent in her denial: She had been cultivating her cornfields at the time, and corn was corn; she could not see how corn could be anything else. My mother had an unflappable bearing even under the severest of conditions.

Without my being preoccupied with study and exams, my mind begins to wander. I fear that my mother's house might fall, but mostly I fear for my brother out there in the cold of the mountains, and the fear is not made any less by the memory of his reassuring laughter the night he came home to bid me to do well. That visit was vintage Wallace—he was always doing the unexpected, at least in my eyes. There was that time when, through my child's eyes, I had seen him as a scholar, because he studied the whole night, his feet in a basin full of cold water. But then he turned out to be a woodworker, and whenever in the Bible I read of Joseph, the father of Jesus, a carpenter, I thought of Good Wallace. And now he had given up everything, his workshop, the second-hand car he had just bought, his wife and child, for the rough life of a freedom warrior. In reality, I had never seen Wallace as a warrior. To me he had always seemed vulnerable, and though he was considerably older than me, I had always felt protective toward him.

There was a man about my brother's age who, because of the manner of his dress, gait, speech, and name—Mũturi, "Ironsmith," which sounded menacing—I always felt could beat him in a physical confrontation. I was then in Kamandũra school. I wanted to warn my brother against the man's company, especially after I learned that they were acquainted, but I did not know how to begin. I approached the subject gingerly, asking him whether they had met recently, as if I was merely interested in knowing about him. But my brother did not seem to be bothered about Mũturi one way or another, and he would ask me to concentrate on my studies and stop worrying about the whereabouts of grown-ups. His indifference to the danger I saw clearly in my mind alarmed me even more, and I never stopped being concerned until the day I heard Kahanya congratulating my brother on how he had floored Mũturi in a street fight.

Similar anxieties now revolve around Kahanya. He will surely betray my brother, and I have no way of warning Wallace about his friend's treachery. But how could friends betray one another? Ngandi, who had seemed to know everything including what happened in the mountains; yes,

Ngandi who had told us stories of the exploits of Dedan Kĩmathi, Stanley Mathenge, and General China with details as if from an eyewitness, should surely be able to explain this. He might even know how to send a message to the mountains. But he never comes to my brother's place anymore. Perhaps I should search for him and, I hope, by chance, run into him in the streets, but I remind myself that I am not supposed to discuss my brother's whereabouts with anybody. Well, I never see him again. I have to sort out these contradictions alone.

I start looking for news and information actively on my own instead of waiting for it to come to me. I have no money for newspapers. I set about collecting odd pieces of printed paper wherever I find them. The Indian shops are the best source. The shopkeepers often use newspapers to wrap sugar or other foods and goods for their customers. Even at dump sites I collect a page here, a page there, some torn, but occasionally I get some in succession. The news is not necessarily current. I have no choice in the matter. All I want is to connect things the way Ngandi used to link local, national, and world events. The stories of Mau Mau as atavistic, anti-progress, antireligion, antimodernity are deeply at odds with what I know of my brother, attested by his last daring act of coming home to wish me well. Other stories are mostly about government victories, enumerating the Mau Mau guerrillas killed, hanged, or captured, the most prominent being General China earlier in the year, mid-January.

The one constant source of consolation is the absence of my brother's name among the fallen. I want him to return home in victory the way Kabae had come home from the Second World War. But there is no printed news of Mau Mau victories, the kind that Ngandi used to tell in very convincing detail. Nor do I find stories of support from abroad such as Ngandi claimed was offered by Egypt, Ethiopia, Russia, and European capitals including London. The only bits I get from London are of a visit by some MPs and of colonial secretaries Oliver Lyttelton and Alan Lennox-Boyd changing places. Otherwise Churchill is still in power, and he sends in more British battalions while recalling others. Other pieces simply confront me with the past of Operation Anvil, the devilish scheme by General Erskine to displace thousands of the Gĩkũyũ, Embu, and Meru from Nairobi, as the colonial state had earlier done with those in the Rift Valley. Limuru, being close to Nairobi, feels the effects of Operation Anvil throughout the year, as it had the effects of other turmoils in the capital. I am heartened when I come across news of the defeat of the French forces in Indochina by a General Giap, at Dien Bien Phu, at about the same time Operation Anvil was playing out, and I hope Kĩmathi would achieve the same kind of victory against the British. Then my brother would come home. In another piece I learn that Eisenhower, through something called Brown versus Board of Education, has ordered the end of segregation of schools in America. It does not make sense to me because I have never seen or even dreamt of the possibility of a school in which African, Asian, and European students coexisted. In Limuru, the Asian school is walled around with stone, an enclosed space behind the shops. The school is part of the

shopping center. I have never seen any Indian student running six miles barefoot to school. As for European schools,
they are invisible. I have never come across any.

Piecing this and that together to make a coherent story
the way Ngandi did is difficult: It is like assembling a jigsaw
puzzle with some pieces missing. It may have been the same
for Ngandi, but he replaced the missing pieces with his fer-
tile imagination. It is okay if I don't reach the level of the
master narrator, I comfort myself, because I don't have to
tell my stories to listeners eager to eat from the palm of
my hand. Still, I try out my knowledge and narrative skills
on Kenneth. But Kenneth does not swallow just anything:
He contests everything that comes out of my mouth, exposing serious gaps in my reporting of events in Kenya and
abroad. But trying to make sense of what's around me, inde-
pendently, and then defending its veracity as well as I can
against Kenneth's skepticism, makes me feel that much
more a man, my own man.

It was about this time that death first danced around
me. It happened after I resumed my friendship with
Ndũng'ũ, my other brother-by-initiation. He had dropped
out of school and did not share the anxiety of waiting for
exam results. But although he was a dropout, Ndũng'ũ had a
very sharp mind, an active intelligence that years later, after
independence, would lead him to become one of the most
successful businessmen in Limuru, a landowner and a town
councilor. At the time, however, people shook their heads
with concern about his future.

Being a man meant that I was an adult able to make decisions on my own. I could sleep out without reporting to my parents. But my mother would not let go of her motherly concern for my welfare, and she kept tabs on the company I kept. A single mother, she did not want to deal with endless conflicts with neighbors. She was of the view that the effective way to avoid such conflicts was to keep to ourselves or else choose friends wisely. She did not object to my friendship with Ndũng'ũ for he was also a relative, but she was somehow aware of all my movements.

Before Kĩmũchũ's execution, he had built an L-shaped house of stone walls and a corrugated iron roof. The house was largely empty because Ndũng'ũ's stepmother usually slept in their shop at the Limuru marketplace. Ndũng'ũ occupied the room at the shorter side of the L shape, and that is where I also spent the night sometimes. For me he was good company, and he was certainly more worldly, especially when it came to girls.

It was very cold that month. We never opened the windows. We used a charcoal burner for heating the room. But on a particularly chilly night, we kept on adding more charcoal, and when we lay on the bed we did not take the burner outside or open the windows. Gradually I sank into a deep sleep. Sometime in the morning, Ndũng'ũ heard a faint knocking at the door and at the windows. He found the will to crawl on the floor and somehow manage to open the door before collapsing, like a drugged person, on the floor where I also lay hardly conscious. But the fresh air must have done something, because when I opened my eyes my mother was standing at the door. To this day I don't know how we fell off the bed onto the floor. Ndũng'ũ and I were saved from asphyxiation just in time.

My mother was very quiet as I followed her back to our house. Later she explained how she had felt ill at ease that it was late in the morning and I had not come home. Fearing that I might have been arrested by the Home Guards, she walked to Ndũng'ũ's place to find out. She was aghast when she saw me on the floor by a charcoal burner that was still burning.

I realized the depth of her shock at the sight of me lying there when later I learned that her first daughter, her first-born, had fallen in a fire and had died of severe burns. It explained why she had always uncharacteristically overreacted whenever she found my younger brother and me, when we were children, playing near a fire or holding a burning piece of wood.

My mother's instincts always amazed me. I remembered that other time when she came to King George VI Hospital when I most needed her. And now she had saved us from carbon monoxide poisoning. Thereafter she would not want to hear anything about my sleeping inside a stone-walled house.

Kenneth, my other brother-by-initiation, and I often met to argue about the world, but mostly to compare notes about our performance and wonder about the exam results, commiserating now and then with one another. But after days of this, we told ourselves that it was better to forget about the exams. So we resumed our interrupted arguments about writing and being sent to prison, both of us still holding firmly to our respective positions. He would remind me that he would write the book that would prove me wrong. But he would not commit as to whether he had already started or when he would. So the arguments continued, about books, about the country, about the world. We never seemed to agree on anything, and yet we still met and argued.

On Sundays he and I went to church in Kamandŭra. He carried a small English-language Bible, which we shared. The preacher would read from the Gĩkŭyŭ-language Bible and we would follow him in the English. We understood Gĩkŭyŭ perfectly, we could also read Gĩkŭyŭ fluently, but somehow it felt more and more natural for us to do it that way.

One Sunday in December 1954, instead of going home after attending the Kamandŭra church, we decided to go to an afternoon open-air service in Ndeiya, about six miles away from home. Open-air services, held after the more formal services inside the church, were becoming the practice on Sundays. The events were not identified with any one particular church denomination. A personal relationship with God was emphasized more than denominational affiliations. These services were more like revival meetings, where even the laypeople could stand up and contribute to the sermons and the prayers.

They coincided with a fundamentalist revival movement that had swept the country since just before the state of emergency was declared. Now the trend seemed to intensify almost as an alternative to the colonial state and the Mau Mau. "Jesus is my personal Savior" was the refrain of many of its adherents. Young people were swept off their feet, and I recall how girls after being saved would give away their earthly adornments such as bead necklaces and earrings. For those who came from more affluent families and saw themselves as modern, being saved gave them freedom to be in the company of others, even men, because Jesus would not let them fall victim to earthly temptations. I don't know why they sang in Luganda, *Tukutendereza Yesu, Yesu we Mlokozi* (we praise Jesus, Jesus the savior), but it may have been because that particular wave of fundamentalism had origins in Uganda and Rwanda. Concerns and restrictions resurfaced when unwanted and unplanned pregnancies became a little bit more frequent among them and no amount of confession and blaming the devil allayed parental concerns.

These open-air Sunday services were also popular because they were among the very few public gatherings that did not need a license from the state. If anything, they met with state approval for they were about Jesus not Kenyatta, about spiritual deliverance from evil and not political liberation from colonial ills.

It was a sunny day, and the service and the singing were good. Some preachers had a way of interpreting some verses in the Bible that made sense of what was happening around us. The signs of war and strife and hunger and false prophets were foretold in the Bible as preceding Christ's Second Coming. Some of the sermons and songs uplifted my soul, freeing me from the anxieties I was carrying.

It was midafternoon when we started our journey back, but instead of going the way we had come, we decided to take what we thought was a shortcut through Ngũirũbi forest. I don't know if we were discussing the service or arguing about writing, or about my narratives gathered from bits of newspapers, but whatever the case, we suddenly heard the order to stop.

In front of us was a white military officer in camouflage gear, pointing a gun at us. He motioned us to put our hands on top of our heads and walk slowly to where others were gathered. It was then that we saw ahead of us people sitting on their haunches, their hands behind their heads. The officer was not alone. On either side of the forest I detected the many eyes of more military personnel. Others guarded the seated crowd with guns and an Alsatian dog. As we sat down, we saw that many of those being held, like us, had been at the religious service. A greenish military vehicle and a smaller one, a jeep, were parked next to the woods, a few yards from the group. Kenneth and I had been caught in a notorious mass screening dragnet.

People who were questioned were assigned to one of three groups: the bad, the worse, and the worst. The group of the worst was being guarded by the fat white officer with the Alsatian dog that looked menacing, panting as if thirsting for blood. Even at a distance the animal revived the terror I had experienced with Kahahu's dog. When Kenneth's turn came, he was placed among the bad. How was a white man able to look a person in the face and decide to which group the person belonged? I discovered the answer to the question when my turn came. By the jeep was some kind of tent in which sat a man wrapped from top to bottom in a white sheet, two slits for his eyes. This was the dreaded *gakũnia*, the man in the hood. Having a pair of faceless eyes peering at you from behind a sheet was chilling. I took it that after they finished with me, they would put me in Kenneth's group since, like him, I was clearly in school uniform.

But to my surprise I was put in the second category of the worse, who would have to answer more questions. In the second round, the culprits were alloted to the bad or the worst group, the latter to be taken to concentration camps. I kept as calm as I could, but inside I was boiling with fear. I knew the baggage I carried. What would I say if asked about my brother Wallace Mwangi? His last and only visit was vivid in my mind. Had somebody seen him visiting us? And as far as I knew, my mother and my brother's wife had not been questioned about the visit.

I stood in front of the white officer near the hooded man. He asked if I understood English and I said yes, hoping that this would meet with his approval.

"Where have you been?"

"An open-air Christian service."

"Say 'effendi,' " he shouted.

"Effendi."

"Where do you go to school?"

"Kĩnyogori Intermediate School. District Education Board. I have done my KAPE and I am waiting for results."

"Have you got brothers?"

"Yes."

"Say 'effendi,' " he said.

"Yes, effendi."

"How many?"

"My father has four wives. I have about ten. . . ."

"Say 'effendi.' "

"Ten, effendi."

"Are all your brothers at home? What do they do?"

"Two work for the government," I said, thinking of Joseph Kabae and Tumbo, and ignoring the first question. "One of them, Joseph Kabae, was a KAR, a soldier who fought for King George during the Second World War," I added, to impress on him our British connections.

But I had forgotten to say "effendi." I felt rather than saw the blow to my face. I staggered but managed to remain on my feet.

"Say 'effendi'!"

"Yes, effendi!" I said, tears at the edges of my eyelids. I was now a man; I was not supposed to cry. But then a man is supposed to fight back, to defend himself and his own, but I could not summon even a gesture of self-defense.

For some reason he took my refusal to cry or scream as defiance, and he rained more blows on me. I fell down. I didn't know whether I should stand up or remain on the ground, but even this indecision seemed to increase his fury.

"*Simama,* stand up."

I stood up, trembling with terror, especially when I saw the officer with the dog coming toward us, as if it was now his turn to deal with me. He said something to my tormentor and then went back to his herd. They may have consulted about something that had nothing to do with me, but I remained fearful.

My tormentor spoke with the hooded man for a while. Then he came back to me.

"Do you have any brothers not at home?"

Butterflies in my tummy. Shall I tell a lie? I decided to stall to buy time.

"I beg your pardon, effendi! What did you say?"

"Have you got brothers not at home?"

There was no point in stalling or telling a lie. I would tell a truthful lie and stick to it.

"I have one who is not there, effendi."

"His name?"

"Wallace Mwangi."

"Effendi!"

"Effendi!"

"Where is he?"

I recalled my mother's admonition.

"I don't know, effendi. I understand he ran away," I said.

"Where to?"

"I was in school when he ran away, and nobody knows where he is."

"Does he come to visit?"

"No, effendi," I said without any hesitation. I was thinking of adding that we feared the government had killed him, but I stopped myself.

He had a further consultation with the hooded man. Apparently, my admitting knowledge of the little bit that was publicly known about my brother had saved the day. When he came back, he motioned me to move to the group of the bad ones who were soon allowed to leave.

I was shaken by the ordeal, but I felt a little pride at not having cried. Kenneth and I walked in silence, not daring to look back. Even when we heard shots and screams behind us, we did not look back. I never knew what happened to the ones who were left behind. We could only guess, but we kept our surmises to ourselves.

It was clear, however, that the man behind the hood was a Limuru resident, probably a neighbor of the very people he was sending to camps or to their deaths. Though shaken I was relieved that I had not been forced to say more than I had.

Kenneth and I did not have much to say about what had just happened or anything else. Such scenes with varying details were common, but this was the first time we were among the dramatis personae. That we had been treated differently may have produced some distance between us and contributed to our silence. Lost in our own thoughts, we did not realize that we had only one more ridge to climb and then we would be home. But both of us needed time to come to terms with what we had witnessed.

It was still early in the afternoon and we decided to take a detour to Manguo to see if Mr. Kĩbicho, the headmaster, could lend us books, even though we were no longer students at his school. Staff houses had not yet been put up at Kĩnyogori, so the teachers stayed in their old houses at Manguo. Although the cover we gave ourselves was books, at the back of our minds we hoped that Mr. Kĩbicho might be able to tell us something, anything, about our exams. He was not at home. We had forgotten that during vacations he normally went back to his home in Nyeri.

Disappointed, we took the path that passed by the house of the deputy headmaster, Stephen Thiro, who must have seen us through the window, because he came to the door and called out to us. He invited us inside. After the ordeal of the day, it was nice to have a cup of tea in our teacher's house.

"Kenneth," he started, smiling, "you have passed the exams."

It was sudden, unexpected. What about me? I thought. But he would not look at me.

"But we don't know what high school you have been admitted to," he continued, his eyes still on Kenneth.

I don't know if Kenneth was happy or not. But my tummy muscles were tight. Had I failed?

"And you, you have been accepted at Alliance High School," he told me, breaking into a broad smile. "Alliance High School announces its admissions earlier than other schools."

I don't know how to take the day with its extreme of downs and ups. The news does not sink in. I don't know how to enjoy it. Even when I go home and say that I have passed the KAPE and have been accepted at Alliance High School, my mother has only one question: Is that the best? And I cannot say what I really want to say—that it is more, it is much more than I had expected. In fact, Alliance High School was not my choice; Mr. Kĩbicho must have inserted the school as one of my choices on my application forms. The others, my brother's wife, my sisters, and my younger brother, are all hearing of this Alliance High School for the first time. But they are happy that I have passed and that I am going to a high school. Word spreads in the region. I am the only one from the entire Limuru area who has been admitted to Alliance High School that year. But slowly, ever so slowly, I make peace with my fate, especially after Reverend Stanley Kahahu comes to my mother's to say that I have done well. It sinks in when later I go to see Mr. Kĩbicho and he congratulates me and tells me that Alliance High School is the best high school in the country, that it admits only the best, before he gives me the package containing information about tuition, clothes, and other items.

And then the brute reality. My mother cannot afford the tuition and everybody knows it. The brother who would have been in a position to help is now in the mountains! Rumors start that the rich and the loyalists would surely petition the government to prevent the brother of a Mau Mau guerrilla from going to such a prestigious high school. I don't know how to take the rumors, which are only adding to my uncertainty. Why, why would anyone want to gang up against me when I have worked so hard to get this far? I recall all the days and nights when I had read or done my homework in flickering firelight, the nights I could not read because we had run out of firewood and paraffin.

Aid comes unexpectedly from someone I would never have imagined: Njairũ, a government-appointed headman with a reputation for being a hard taskmaster, an enforcer with a vengeance of communal labor and attendance at *barazas*, the well-known leader of the hated Home Guard squad who would kill my brother on sight. He puts an end to the rumor. No force will stop me from going to Alliance High School, he says. He personally goes to all my half brothers to impress upon them the importance of what I have done. Some give their shares freely. Njairũ leans heavily on the few who are reluctant.

Donations come in here and there, and eventually I have the required initial payment but not enough for a whole year. This is fine for the time being; we shall cross the other bridges when we come to them. I have a new set of clothes and a wooden box. I have got everything I need, well, almost everything. A pair of shoes and long stockings are among the requirements, and I cannot find the money for them. One can ask donations for big things like tuition: Education has always been seen as a personal and communal ideal. But money for shoes and stockings?

I had never owned or worn a pair in my life, except once when I tried on my elder brother's shoes and trousers, all bigger than my size, and he caught me strutting about in the yard, my younger brother crying for his turn. But after I was admonished rather harshly, my younger brother laughed at me. Otherwise I had walked barefoot all my life. The expectation of wearing shoes for the first time was as intense as that other time long ago when my mother bought me my first shirt and shorts for my primary school at Kamandūra. A pair of shoes stands between me and high school.

My sister Njoki comes to the rescue. Njoki is the quietest in my mother's house. She broods a lot. Life has not treated her well. There was a time when she was in love with a tractor driver from Ngeca. He was part of the workforce in the construction of the Limuru tunnel under the land owned by a Mr. Buxton, one of the soldiers who settled in the area after the First World War. Before the tunnel, the train took a long time to go around the hill. The digging of the tunnel after the Second World War had created all sorts of rumors—that the whites were interfering with the order of nature, that they were planning something sinister for Africans. Otherwise why was the whole thing so secret? Still, there was a certain prestige conferred on those who worked on the project, especially the drivers. My sister was happy when her tractor driver visited our place and talked of the dynamite used to break up the rocks. He talked of the dangers he faced daily and even said that some people had been killed by the rocks and dynamite. The danger he toiled under and his bravery captivated Njoki even more. She was so much more alive: She used to laugh and dance. But her love did not meet the approval of my brother Wallace. He and his friends dissuaded her from the wedding of her choice; she instead married a wealthier suitor who owned a truck and had a contract to supply murram for road repair. The marriage had grown sour and ended in divorce. She had lost her first love, the tractor driver, in the process. News of his death under falling rock in the tunnel together with her failed marriage took the joy of life from her. Laughter left her. She earned money, not much, by working in the tea plantations across the rail or in Kahahu's pyrethrum fields.

Now she gives up all she has to buy me the required pair of shoes and stockings. I am moved by this. Instead of saying thank you, I tell her that I am very sorry for the day I once chased her through the pyrethrum field with a chameleon on a stick. Like many others in the area, she was mortally afraid of chameleons. I had always felt guilty about the incident, but she obviously has forgotten all about it, and it takes some seconds for her to understand what I am talking about. And then she breaks into laughter. A big bellyful of laughter. It is so wonderful to see her smile, to see the gloom disappear from her face, to see how beautiful she really is, and whenever I wear shoes I shall always recall that smile and laughter.

I pack everything in the wooden box. Alliance High School is a boarding school: I will be coming home only during the holidays. I am ready to go. I wish I had a way of saying farewell to Wallace Mwangi, my brother who is out in the cold of the mountains, but no doubt he will get the news the same way he knew about my exams at Loreto.

There are two other people I must see before I go. My grandfather. Regardless of whatever has happened between us, he is still the only grandfather I have, and I am named after him. His daughter is my mother, but she is also my symbolic daughter. It is in the afternoon, and he is sitting in an armchair on the verandah of his house. He asks Mũkami to bring me a chair. She does and follows this with a glass of hot milk. I tell him the news, but I also know he knows because I have been the talk of the region for weeks. I feel as if my visit also relieves him of a weight inside.

But you will be coming to see us during your holidays, he says. And then unable to hide his feelings, he breaks into a smile, and calls out to his wife, loudly, I knew he could read. He could write what was in my mind exactly. He gave robes to my thoughts. Go well. Continue holding the pen firmly. He makes as if to spit on his breast, a gesture of showers of blessing. Then he tells Mũkami to bring "that parcel," which turns out to be his wallet. He gives me some money to buy myself something on the way to my new school. I feel good. He had once trusted me and my abilities enough to make me his scribe and bird of good omen.

The other person? My father! Though I haven't admitted it to myself, I am haunted by a sense of alienation, and I still carry within me the ugly image of our last encounter. I have to see him: I don't know what words will pass between us, but a fleeting thought has suddenly become an irresistible desire. When I set foot on the compound, the same compound that was my playground for the first half of my childhood, I feel my heart skip a beat. I am returning to the old homestead for the very first time since my expulsion. My mother's former hut is still standing, but now green plants have sprouted on the roof and all around the walls, loudly announcing abandonment. My mind races back to beginnings, to the games of my childhood. It is a sunny day, but for some reason what comes to mind is the song we used to sing to welcome rain. At the muffled sound of raindrops on the thatched roofs, we would run out to the compound.

> Rain, I ask you to fall
> I shall offer you a bull
> With a bell around his neck
> That sings ding-dong ding-dong

Images upon images of the past. Tears and laughter. All the siblings who are at home welcome me and crowd around me. First I enter Wangarĩ's hut, the senior wife's house, and before I have even uttered a word, Wabia, my blind half sister, says: Is that Ngũgĩ? Yes, it's me, I say, with a smile she cannot see, but a smile offered broadly. Here in this hut was the scene of the nightly performance of stories, riddles, and proverbs and the discussion of national and world affairs.

Wangarĩ is sorry that she has nothing for me to eat, but she could make me a type of porridge she used to make for me. No, no, it is not necessary. I say farewell to her and to Wabia. Then I go to the second wife's house, my second mother, Gacoki. She is not a woman of many words, she is still her shy self, but she ventures to ask, Is this Alliance in another country? It is only a manner of speaking, she is just happy that I have come to visit. And lastly I go to Njeri's house. She is her same, strong-boned, talkative self, admonishing me for not having sent word in advance that I was coming, and now unprepared she has nothing to give me to eat. But she offers eggs that I could take with me to school. No, no, I say, thinking of the days of Bono Mayai.

Finally I turn to my father. He is sitting on a stool inside Njeri's hut. My father has nothing to say beyond, You have done well and you have my blessings. I know that he has been receiving many congratulations from other elders on the achievement of his son, but embarrassment prevents him from saying more. I know that he has nothing material to give me and he does not even make a gesture. He is really down and out. But I am not here for money or gifts from him. I want to give myself a gift. I do not want to start a new life with resentment in my heart. My visit is my way of telling him that even though he has not asked for forgiveness, I still forgive him. Like my mother, I believe that anger and hatred corrode the heart. I want my actions to speak for me, positive deeds to be my only form of vengeance. Not much is spoken. But as I am about to leave, he stands up and walks a few steps with me. Then he does something I have never seen him do: He takes me up the dump site, telling me to be careful of the stinging plants, the kind we called *thabai*. We stand there looking down the slope I had known so well, the slope where I often witnessed my sisters and brothers and mothers going on their way to work at the white-owned tea plantations and scattering all over. From this hill one could hear the sirens from the Limuru Bata Shoe Company built in 1938. And for all those years, the siren, *king'ora*, had become a timekeeper, marking the passage of the day for all of us: The morning siren announced the break of day, the midday one, lunch break, and the last one, nightfall. We talk about the before and after of the sirens. This was the same hill from which my mother claimed she had witnessed Indian ghosts holding lights in their hands and walking about in the dark. Yes, so many memories, of being stung by stinging nettles, of hiding our dogs in the bush around the dump site and then my mother taking them back to the Indian shops! Even my father is absorbed in thoughts of his own as if surveying the lands that once belonged to him and the distance he has covered since his flight from Mũrang'a. Or his journey in time from his birth before Kenya was Kenya, before there was Nairobi or Limuru or any town beyond the coast; his journey through the First and Second World Wars and now Mau Mau with his sons fighting on both sides of the conflict. I wish I could say to him: Your thoughts about this, Father, but I don't say it. He breaks the silence but not about the past. You have done well, he says at last. The road ahead is long. There will be holes and bumps.

You shall fall sometimes. The thing is to stand up and continue walking. His tone is matter-of-fact. But I have a feeling that he is telling this to himself as well. And in my heart I say thank you. I am free. I am not a prisoner of anger or resentment anymore.

Everything is ready. I have been to see my friend Kenneth. He has been accepted in Kambũi Teacher Training School. So also have Mũrage Chege, Mũturi Ndiba, and Kamĩri Ndotono, all my classmates. Kambũi is Harry Thuku's home area, once the site of the Gospel Missionary Society before it merged with Church of Scotland Mission to form the Presbyterian Church in 1946. Kenneth is disappointed that he has not been admitted into a high school, but he does not forget to bring up our arguments about writing and prison. I will still write that book, he says, just to prove you wrong about the license to write.

My mother is not coming to the train, she tells me. Go well, always do your best, and you will be all right. I discover that Liz Nyambura, a senior at Alliance Girls High School, the girl who was a math prodigy way back in my early Kamandũra days, and Kenneth Wanjai wa Jeremiah, already in form two at Alliance High School, are returning to Kikuyu the same day. I join them at the railway platform. My sisters, my brother's wife, and my younger brother accompany me to the station.

The platform seems very busy, but probably not as busy

as in those days long ago when the Limuru railway platform was a social center. I recall the days when my sisters and brother used to run down the slope from our father's house to meet the twelve o'clock passenger train to Kampala or Kisumu. Oh, how I used to envy them, wishing for the day when I would become an adult so that I could race other young men and women to the railway station! And now I am there, not to see the train come and go but to ride it.

All the people present assume that I am excited because of my next school; only my younger brother knows what I am really feeling. For the first time in my life I am going to board a passenger train. I recall that time when I was not able to board a train to Elburgon. I recall how my brother, who took the train then, would later hint at the wonders of the train ride as a way of letting me know that he had one up on me. He knew that I was envious of his achievement. But he does not know that I have also been envious of John and Joan, the fictional schoolkids who lived in Oxford but went to school in Reading by train. Now my time has come. Now I am doing the same thing. A train to school. A boarding school. Alliance High School, Kikuyu. Twelve miles away, but it is as if I'm about to ride a train to paradise. This one is even more special. It will carry my dreams in a time of war.

At long last the train arrives. We walk toward the coaches that are not marked for Europeans only or Asians only. Third class is not even dignified by "Africans only." Wanjai and Liz and others enter and as they do they show a piece of paper to a European railway official. It is now my turn. The official stops me. Pass? What pass? He demands to see a pass that allows me to move from Limuru to Kikuyu, only twelve miles away. It is a new law under the state of emergency. No member of the Gĩkũyũ, Embu, and Meru community can board the train without a government-issued pass. But nothing of the sort was mentioned on any of the information sheets in the package from the school. Interventions by Wanjai and Liz Nyambura are to no avail. The only assurance Wanjai can give is that he will tell the school about the mishap. But his words don't touch me; they can't heal the wound in my heart. By now there is a commotion around me, different people offering different opinions.

I stand there on the platform with my luggage and watch the train move away with my dreams but without me, with my future but without me, till it disappears. I shed tears. I don't want to, I am a man, I am not supposed to cry, but I cannot help it. The white military officer who had floored me with blows could not make me cry; but this white officer, a railway official, who has denied me a ride in the train has done it. Those who would have commiserated with me are themselves in need of commiseration. I don't know how my mother will receive this, for mine was also her dream.

And then out of nowhere an African assistant station master arrives on the scene. Somebody must have gone to appeal to him. His name, I will learn, is Chris Kahara. Years later, after independence, he will become Chairman of the Kenya Pipeline Company. But just now he is simply an assistant station master in his official white uniform, a white safari jacket over white trousers. He tells me not to cry; he will do his best to ensure that I get to Kikuyu. Only I will probably miss the bus to school. But I could run through the Ondiri marshes to my dreams. Before he has finished talking, along comes a goods train. It is not the smooth-looking passenger train I had hoped for, but I follow him to the last car. He has made arrangements. I get into the car. I am surrounded by workmen's tools and clothes. I can smell their sweat but it does not matter. The car has no windows so I don't see the landscape. The journey feels like one of a thousand miles. I am numb with fear that something will happen to stop me from catching up to my dreams.

At last I arrive at Kikuyu station. Like Limuru, it was opened in 1899. Somebody opens the back doors for me, behaves as if he is simply checking the tools, mumbles something like "It is here," and I jump out, with my box. The man smiles, closes the door, and walks away.

I stand there at the station platform and watch the goods train go by, this time with relief and gratitude. I look around and see some shops. I take my box and drag it toward them. I cannot believe that this is the real Kikuyu Township. It consists of two rows of Indian shops very much like those at Limuru, but far fewer. But I am not interested in the Indian traders behind the counters or the African shoppers. I may have overcome one obstacle, but I have another to worry about.

The information sheet that I had received stated that a school bus would meet students at the station. I am late. The bus must have come and gone without me. I have no idea about the distance to and location of the school. I approach a stranger who looks askance at me and then points to a road, mumbling something about going past the Ondiri marshes, and walks away. I will have to wade through the Ondiri marshes the way I used to do in Manguo, except that then I carried nothing heavier than a bird's egg or a bundle of wet clothes. Now I have a box with my belongings. And then I recall the story of Ondiri that I had read in *Mwendwa nĩ Irĩ* and Ngandi's stories about people disappearing in the bog never to be seen again. Was this the same Ondiri? No, I am not going to walk through the Ondiri bog, no matter what. I will stick to the road.

I am about to start walking toward the road pointed out to me by the stranger when the school bus comes for others on the Mombasa train, which also arrives at that moment. I walk toward it. The teacher, who I learn later is the acting principal, Mr. James Stephen Smith, checks my name on his list and tells me to enter, as the other students do the same.

It is only after I enter the bus and sit down that I let out a sigh of relief and dare to look ahead. A new world. Another journey. A few minutes later, at a junction off the Kikuyu road, I see a billboard with banner letters so personal that I think it must have been for me alone. WELCOME TO ALLIANCE HIGH SCHOOL. I hear my mother's voice: Is it the best you can do? I say to her with all my heart, Yes, Mother, because I also know what she really is asking for is my renewal of our pact to have dreams even in a time of war.

Irvine, California
February 12, 2009

Limuru Station

Acknowledgments

Thanks to Njeri wa Ngũgĩ, who suggested this; Gloria Loomis, who told me it cannot wait; Kĩmunya, my general assistant in Kenya; Kenneth Mbũgua, who provided pictures and information about our school days; Charity W. Mwangi, who gave information on Kĩambaa and Banana Hills; Neera Kapila for information on railroad stations; and, as always, my assistant Barbara Caldwell, for library and Internet research and editorial work.

www.vintage-books.co.uk